Personal Finances for Ministers

PERSONAL FINANCES FOR MINISTERS

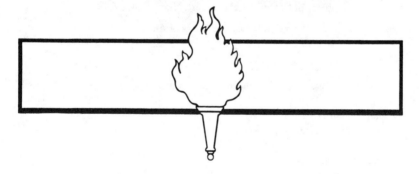

Darold H. Morgan

BROADMAN PRESS
Nashville, Tennessee

Library of Congress Cataloging-in-Publication Data

Morgan, Darold H., 1924-
    Personal finances for ministers.

    (Broadman leadership series)
    Bibliography: p.
    1. Clergy—Finance, Personal.   I. Title.
II. Series.
BV4397.M66   1985   332.024′2   85-17443
ISBN 0-8054-6405-0

To the staff of the Annuity Board, a group of dedicated women and men who are genuinely interested in helping pastors and their families

Acknowledgments

One of the major reasons I left the active pastorate fifteen years ago to work at the Annuity Board of the Southern Baptist Convention was to encourage ministers and their families to participate in the benefit programs. I still believe pastors can work more effectively at the major tasks of evangelism, missions, and church administration when they and their families have solid insurance and retirement protection.

Discovering that some ministers today are sharpening their money management skills is reassuring. Others are not. This book is designed to help ministers regardless of where they are in the pilgrimage of service.

The staff of the Annuity Board has assisted immeasurably with this book. Not to have drawn on the extraordinary skills of this group for their expertise in legal, technical, tax, investment, and marketing fields would have been shortsighted. John D. Bloskas rightly deserves singling out for creative editing and assistance. I doubt if the book would have emerged without his encouragement. Ileen Bray, Margaret Ward, and the word processing staff at the Annuity Board also deserve special commendation for their competent help.

My hope and prayer is that these pages will give many more ministers the joy and satisfaction of good money management.

Introduction

An attractive young couple stopped at the exhibit booth of the Annuity Board, the pension board of the Southern Baptist Convention, during one of our national meetings. I listened as they introduced themselves, supposing to myself that they were going to ask the usual questions regarding insurance and retirement plans. They wanted more however. "Do you have any material that will help us with our personal financial planning?" The young couple said they had just completed their seminary training and were expressing a concern which they had developed there. "We have heard many horror stories about preachers who have been over their heads in debt," they said. "Do you have any advice for us so we won't end up in debt?"

Later at the same Convention, I was talking with a longtime friend who was planning to retire at the end of the year. He spoke of the anticipation and satisfaction that he and his wife were feeling as they neared the end of their many years of active service in the ministry. As he contemplated his position, he said he felt good about his future. They did not have any large indebtedness. They owned a lovely home which was paid for because, during the time of their last two pastorates, the churches provided them a housing allowance that helped financially. He commented that his retirement income was above average, again because of the care and concern of his churches.

As we talked, I thought, *Here is a pastor who should have some good advice for young couples just beginning their ministries.* I mentioned the couple who had sought information earlier and asked, "What would you tell that young preacher?"

The older minister responded with enthusiasm. What he said can apply to everyone, regardless of where he is in his career path. "Tell him," he said, "to set goals immediately in financial planning and to stick with them through the years. My wife and I started out that way and, believe me, we are glad today that we did."

I have pondered at length the questions asked by the young couple and the response given by the older minister. Although the two couples are years apart in age, the need for planning is common to both. Yet financial planning for the young couple will be considerably different from that of the older minister who is about to retire. Each must plan from his own perspective. By perspective I mean viewing life from where one is in his career path.

Are you just starting the exciting pilgrimage as a minister? Have you been a minister for several years or maybe even ten or twenty years? Are you nearing retirement? Consider where you are now, decide where you want to be, then initiate the plan of action you believe will take you there. Planning is essential in each phase of your career. The key always is to *plan early,* then discipline yourself!

Once you begin, update your plans by reviewing them periodically. Review them with your spouse. Review them with all family members. Make sure they have input.

This book presents a guide for a minister of the gospel to evaluate his financial standing, then to establish a plan of action for reaching financial goals. In so doing, the minister must realize that he has a series of challenges somewhat unlike those of the laity. For example, Social Security treats the minister as self-employed; housing, a major part of anyone's budget, is usually determined by the church; however, salaries and allowances are often far below average. But all of these will yield to planning. Financial management for the minister is biblical, practical, professional, and imperative.

Contents

1

Who Is the Minister?

At the outset, some current definitions of a gospel minister demand attention. The dictionary definition of a minister is a person who is authorized to carry out the spiritual functions of a church: to conduct worship, to preach, and to administer the sacraments. The word *gospel* means good news or a message, teaching, doctrine, or course of action having certain efficacy. *Gospel*, when used in a Christian sense, means the teachings of Jesus Christ and His apostles. Each denomination expresses its own criteria for interpreting the holy calling of the minister. A gospel minister generally functions as a spiritual leader to bring Christ's teachings to a congregation.

Identifying the Minister

In all denominations, the range of ages and experience of ministers is wide. Newly graduated seminarians, preachers in their thirties, forties, fifties, and those close to retirement encompass the persons called ministers.

In recent years a very large group known as bivocational ministers has emerged. These persons have incomes from two or more sources, the larger one coming from a secular enterprise. Some bivocational pastors earn incomes well beyond the average minister's income. Others actually need a second income to keep the proverbial "wolf away from the door."

These ministers, from the young seminarian to the seasoned veteran to the bivocational, need guidance in financial planning whether they do the work themselves or have a financial planner do it for them. A guide designed specifically for the minister must take into account the wide range of ages and financial income differences of these persons. This variance is true with all professional groups.

Without exception, ministers have unique demands placed upon them and their families when it comes to financial matters. They must be aware constantly of their impression on others concerning spending money and paying their bills promptly. They also, in many instances, are at the mercy of the local congregation for housing.

This book is written with five specific ministers in mind. Naturally, the names have been changed, but each is a real person. Each was chosen because he represents the changing seasons in the life of a minister. These seasons confirm the obvious fact that the financial needs of pastors vary. Perhaps the best way to understand this is to look at each minister.

The New Seminary Graduate

David S., twenty-eight years of age, married and just moved to the seminary where he enrolled. His wife, Mary, accepts David's commitment to the pastoral ministry and deeply supports him. Both David and Mary planned to earn seminary degrees, but the pressures of economic realities demanded that Mary work, so she dropped her classes after the first semester.

Income from Mary's job, the money David earned from part-time work, and checks from their parents got them through seminary with a minimum of indebtedness. A frugal life-style made them keenly aware of the things they needed but were willing to postpone in order to complete his education.

During the final semester, two events altered their lives: their first child was born, and a call came for their first full-time pastorate in a small city about two hundred miles from their hometown. David was most appreciative for this call because many of his friends were not immediately called or assigned to a church. He recalled reading about a surplus of ministers in some denominations. One reason for this is the extraordinarily large number of older students entering the seminaries. Another reason is the large number of retired pastors who continue to serve while drawing Social Security and denominational retirement incomes.

David's salary was more than he expected, and he also had the use of the church parsonage. After struggling through school with very little money to meet his family's needs, David was impressed with this abundance. He was aware of and grateful for what his church was providing. The committee from the church told him they would pay his car expenses and his insurance and provide full protection for retirement. The church would give him a moving allowance which, to a new pastor, was both surprising and welcome.

The day came when David, Mary, and their child moved to the church field. They packed a rented trailer to capacity with the household accumulations of almost four years of marriage. The empty parsonage was cleaned; the pantry was filled with staples which the congregation gave in the beautiful tradition of "the pastor's pounding." Mary was especially pleased with the space— three bedrooms, two baths, and a kitchen with a built-in stove and refrigerator.

The church treasurer visited and told David he would give him a check on the first and fifteenth of each month. David was somewhat perplexed when the treasurer said in the form of a question, "I'll take your tithe out if you want me to?" David responded that one of the joys of his family's Christian responsibilities was writing and giving that check to the Lord, and he preferred to do it.

The first paycheck was the largest one he had ever received. How would he divide it? Of course, to David and his family the tithe came first. Utilities, which were higher than he expected, were next. An amount was set aside to purchase some furniture when they needed it. And there were the clothing needs for the baby, Mary, and himself.

When they finished dividing the check, David and Mary sat in silence in their sparsely furnished living room. After a few minutes Mary said, "Not much is left. What about the other things we need?" They knew they needed help in planning their family budget.

The Middle-Aged Minister

Dr. Robert J. is forty-five years old, married, and has three children, ages twenty, eighteen, and fourteen. He and his wife, Lois, have been in the ministry for almost twenty years. Two of their children are in college. During the past four years, Lois has been teaching school to help with the cost of keeping their children in college. Robert is in the sixth year at the church where he is pastor. It is a suburban church whose growth has been consistent. He and his wife are concerned about their financial situation because they are living in church-owned housing, yet at their age they realize that they should be buying their own home. They have read about the advantages of pastors buying their own homes. Although Robert's salaries from the churches that he has served have been sufficient, the demands of a growing family have taken every cent.

Robert and Lois have other challenges also. They are concerned about their aging parents. Since seminary days, they have never lived nearer than two hundred miles to their parents. Both sets of parents are receiving Social Security benefits as the major part of their retirement incomes. Robert's mother and Lois's father have serious health problems. Though financial demands from both sides have been minimal, frequent visits have been necessary.

College expenses for their sons are high. Both boys work at summer jobs to earn spending money. The older son has a job at school, but the younger one has asked that he not be expected to work his first year so that he can concentrate on getting off to a good start with his studies. He says that he will work during summers and during the school years the remaining time. Both sons drive older cars which always need repairs. The ages of both boys put them in the high risk category for auto insurance. One son attends the state university; the other is studying at a denominational college sixty miles from home.

The financial concerns of this family center around the high costs of education, the need to help aged parents, the growing awareness that they should be purchasing their own home for retirement, and the need to set aside more money for retirement.

Their financial challenges are similar to those of David and Mary. "Where is all the money going?" they ask. Their major needs are related to budget planning, establishing financial goals, and determining their requirements in light of the priorities mentioned.

The Older Minister

William P., age sixty-two, is married to Dorothy, age sixty-one. Married forty years, they have two children, both married, and four grandchildren. They have been in the ministry for more than forty years. He served as a pastor for most of that time; but for the past eight years, he has served in an area of supervision for his denomination.

A couple of years before he assumed the denominational position, he led the church where he served to give him a housing allowance. Their home is now almost debt free.

His present salary is larger than any he had received as a pastor. Demands on his budget are less because the children are educated and married with families of their own. In recent years, he has had tax-sheltered funds from his salary to boost his retirement income and to reduce his income taxes. William considers this one of the best things he and his wife have done in preparing for retirement.

Dorothy never worked outside the home. Her place, she insisted, was at her husband's side, taking care of his needs. Since her father died four years ago, her mother has lived with them. Dorothy stays at home to care for her mother, but they realize that the attention she requires will eventually demand that they move her to a nursing home. Her mother's needs have not affected them financially because her Social Security and savings are adequate.

In three years, William will be sixty-five, normally the time to retire. The couple has several major concerns. Do they want to sell their home and move nearer their children when they retire? (The children live hundreds of miles from them.) Can they afford the rising costs of full-time care for Dorothy's mother? Will they have enough money in their retirement years?

The Bivocational Minister

The fourth group of ministers is represented by George B., who serves in the Midwest. George is forty-seven, and his wife, Eleanor, is three years younger. His family has three incomes. The first is from George's job as a contractor. He specializes in small jobs, such as repairing and painting homes and buildings, and does electrical and plumbing work.

The second income comes from the work Eleanor performs as a clerk in the county courthouse. She began her job when the youngest of their four children entered school. Her salary is adequate for the Midwest area, and she has an excellent health insurance plan which permits her to enroll the entire family as dependents. Their two older children are married and live nearby. The younger children are in public schools and want to go to college someday.

The third income is from George's first love, a small church ten miles away in the country where he serves as pastor. He felt deeply impressed to go into the ministry after he returned home from military service. He and his wife married in their home church before he went into the service. When he discussed with Eleanor his desire to seek ordination, a genuine dilemma emerged. "I didn't marry a preacher," she said. "What will you do about school? How will we raise our family?"

The solution emerged slowly. Both George and Eleanor agreed that it was God's will for George to continue to work as a small job contractor. On Sundays, he would preach in churches near his home. Because of his contacts, his skills in communications, and his basic reputation for mature judgment, he soon was called to a rural church. After serving there several years on a part-time basis, he was called to another small church. Serving the rural church brought him real satisfaction. The small church appreciated him for accepting its call at a relatively low salary.

George and Eleanor own their home. The only retirement they have is from Social Security and the county employee plan in which Eleanor participates. George has never joined a retirement plan. He is thinking now about investing in an individual retirement account with a local savings and loan association.

George is concerned about the accounting demands of his small business. A local accountant who audits his books keeps telling him about the tax advantages he has as an ordained minister and his need for keeping good records. Long-term planning is not one of George's current goals.

The Retired Minister

The last real-life representative of the ministry is seventy-four-year-old Clyde C., who is in his eighth year of retirement. After an active ministry totaling some forty years, Clyde retired and began receiving his retirement benefit from his denominational program at age sixty-five. Later, a small rural church wanted to call him, and he agreed when he learned he could do so without losing any benefits. The church designated the small amount it paid him as automobile expenses and housing allowance. By doing this, he was able to collect his Social Security benefits and denominational pension without any reduction.

Clyde was forced to give up his pulpit when health problems mandated he retire for the second time. His major concern is inadequate retirement income from Social Security and his ministerial retirement account. The small amount is the result of low salaries on which benefits are based. He does not want his children to be obligated to help him and his wife, Eloise, who is two years younger than he. The small but neat home they bought near their daughter is paid for through a small inheritance left to his wife. Medical costs are another concern. Both of them have health problems that require costly medication and regular doctor visits. A noncancelable, Medicare Supplement provides some relief with the bills.

Clyde and Eloise have discovered the peculiar loneliness that the older minister and his spouse face when the moved to a home away from people they know and love. Because they always lived frugally, they have been able to adjust their spending without damaging their self-esteem. They participate in a senior adult program in a church near their home, and they are grateful for this.

From their perspective, the couple has learned that financial planning is just as valid for them in retirement as it was when they first started their career.

Summary

These five ministers represent the spectrum of the ministry—from twenty-eight to seventy-four years of age, from a recent seminary graduation to retirement, from new parents to grandparents, from concerns about getting a living room suite for the first time to the concern of moving out of a large home to a smaller one.

Each of the seasons of the ministry brings the need for in-depth planning for financial management. Perhaps no single professional career is as demanding and changing in financial planning as the minister's. Yet he can take heart in remembering that sound biblical principles support his efforts.

2

Biblical Foundations
for Financial Planning

From where do attitudes about money and its handling come? For ministers, one naturally assumes a biblical basis. Yet in reviewing the ministers mentioned in the first chapter, a variety of sources for personal convictions about money and its use becomes evident.

Two of the ministers speak fondly and gratefully about parents who taught them early in life, by biblical precept and example, that everything they have had is from the Lord. Tithing is signally important. Saving is essential. Living within one's means is good religion, and planning ahead is fine wisdom. These influences have shaped their attitudes toward the handling of money.

Another of them recalls a Bible study hour at church when he was a teenager. A capable teacher developed a long-remembered theme from Malachi 3:10, "Bring ye all the tithes into the storehouse, . . . and prove me now herewith, saith the Lord of hosts, if I will not open you the windows of heaven, and pour you out a blessing, that there shall not be room enough to receive it." The interpretation is simply stated: "You cannot outgive God." The young man has learned that stewardship can be an adventure. Everything one possesses is from God. Give Him all you can. Step out on faith and discover God's sustaining and generous hand. "You cannot outgive God."

In contrast, another minister came to his Christian experience of redemption while a college student. He had no roots in a Christian family, nor did he have years in a church setting. Strangely, in comparison with the others, he responds freely to human needs.

But tithing is an unfamiliar concept to him. On the other hand, his family almost remonstrates with him about his openheartedness. His casual generosity sometimes results in a lack of necessities for family. Impulsiveness often characterizes his response to a need. As yet, he has not developed a workable plan for family finances, but he practices Christian sharing.

In further contrast, another minister under survey is the product of an upper middle-class American home with some conflicting values. His limited financial resources have been a real problem. He needs dollars in too many places. Giving a tenth of his income to the church, pledging to a building campaign beyond the tithe, and responding generously to mission offerings are all very painful to him. He was not reared to be sensitive to such appeals. In his sermon schedule, preaching about biblical principles and stewardship is rare. He and his family still do not have a satisfactory plan for their finances. Yet he does not argue with his family about money management because of painful childhood memories. Both he and his wife are aware that the time for planning is upon them.

Thus not all ministers have a "natural" orientation to the biblical foundations of Christian stewardship. Indeed, some clergymen are even reluctant to think about it, fearing it exposes a lack of faith. Others have warped mindsets from roots in family conflicts over money. Then again, sometimes reluctance emerges because of negative attitudes from self-centered, immature church leaders or from a lack of coherent personal values on money.

Yet, as Christian ministers who must be free of financial anxiety, a biblical perspective of stewardship is essential. The Bible has much to say about the elements of financial planning in both Old and New Testaments. These principles must be brought into fresh perspective because they contain their own thrust of conviction and priority toward motivation. Ministers especially need to keep them in full view since their personal convictions in this area affect both their professional influence and performance.

Defining Biblical Stewardship

A manual on financial planning for ministers must begin with the biblical foundations entailing stewardship. Biblical stewardship touches far more than economics. It puts the whole of existence into perspective. Every phase of life is involved—financial, mental, physical, spiritual, social. This permeation strongly implies that, properly grasped, the principles about biblical stewardship can enrich and shape all segments of life.

Simply stated, biblical stewardship embodies the highest form of responsible living. Lee E. Davis and Ernest D. Standerfer have written effectively in defining Christian stewardship. "For the Christian, to be a steward is to manage responsibly all of one's life, influence, and resources."[1] Add to their definition one by Cecil Ray, and we can see strong theological support. "Christian stewardship is the ordering or shaping of the whole of life in accordance with the will of God as revealed in Jesus Christ."[2]

These definitions focus on one dynamic truth: Responsible Christian stewardship presents a direct corollary to the dual awareness of God's role as both Creator and Redeemer through faith in Jesus Christ. As this relationship permeates all basic Christian truth and practice, it undergirds the full practice of Christian stewardship.

God's Plan in Creation and Redemption

Let's go back to some of the ministers' attitudes that we reviewed. One young man came to Christ in his college years without the roots of a Christian home and the years of training in Sunday School. Another minister, the product of a rather affluent background, is now wrestling with money management in his own home where there simply is not enough money to meet all the needs. Both of these situations cry out for the stabilizing influence found in the biblical principle of divine creation.

God owns everything because He made it. He had a plan in cre-

ation; He has a plan for ultimate consummation. The Bible makes
it clear all things are moving to His final control. In the meantime,
He trusts His children to manage His creation. This is a fundamental truth. If ministers believe the implications of the full biblical doctrine of creation and ultimate fulfillment, it will make a
considerable difference in every phase of their lives, including
money. Christian stewardship apart from this cardinal truth
makes no sense. To implement this principle mandates a plan for
making and spending money.

Now, apply this truth also to the workaday world of a minister.
One man's current plan of financial management consists of impulsive response to the needs that a minister sees. Another well-
known minister has literally catapulted himself with a credit card
into a sizable debt load. He rationalizes that it is all right to be in
debt "because this is the way I was taught in childhood." Yet the
biblical roots of creation and redemption mandate a reappraisal of
planning ahead as God always is planning ahead. However much
we puzzle ourselves about a seemingly senseless world at times,
God has *not* ordered it haphazardly. Creation demonstrates both
plan and purpose in divine sequence.

Richard Cunningham was on target when he said in this connection, *"As sovereign creator and lord, God is owner of everything in
the universe, and he alone has the right to define the nature and purpose of
life and the world he has made."*[3]

For structuring a philosophy of stewardship, one needs more
than a parade of isolated proof texts mandating a rigid code of conduct. Thus one study declares that "stewardship is not primarily a
theological tool for insuring the economic health of the church."[4] It
is far more inclusive. One must notice the continuity of creation
and redemption in both the Old and New Testaments. A. R. Fagan
quoted William Hendricks's observation, "It is the position of the
biblical material, the New Testament assumes it from the Old Testament and builds on it, that all substances and circumstances are
so because God makes them or permits them to be. This is the
Christian doctrine of creation."[5]

When an individual becomes aware of God's goodness and mercy, a sense of stewardship inspires the gracious response. The disciple wants to order his or her life in the light of God's continuing grace.

Stewardship as a Personal Response

True Christian stewardship, then, is a personal response to God, growing out of one's gratitude for God's gift of physical life through creation and spiritual life through His gifts of grace in Jesus Christ. By His grace, He has redeemed us from sin, darkness, guilt, and hopelessness. One of the key concepts in understanding Christian redemption comes from the gift-giver-receiver relationship. "For God so loved the world, that He gave His only begotten Son, that whoever believes in Him should not perish, but have eternal life" (John 3:16, NASB). Paul's exultant cry in his Corinthian correspondence confirms this: "Thanks be unto God for his unspeakable gift" (2 Cor. 9:15).

Christian living at its best is simply a response to God's gift in creation and redemption. All of our lives belong to Him, making us stewards. Our task in life is to manage what belongs to God. All our possessions, time, equipment, and talent are on temporary loan from the God who created and redeemed us. How much all of us would have been helped if we could have learned these lessons as we learned our *ABCs!* Most of us had to acquire these convictions and grasp the attendant applications as adults.

A pastor once told me that one of his main goals in life was to get his wife a mink coat and a Cadillac. They were tired of feeling constantly denied some of life's finer things. I wanted to ask why he felt this was such a major goal in life but decided to rejoice inwardly that his situation would be extremely rare in the ministry. He realized this unusual goal; however, he forfeited his right to experience the higher joy beyond material values. Among other things, his wife wrecked the Cadillac! The real tragedy was that he was consequently unable to lead his church family to any exciting commitment of biblical stewardship. His own values were too shallow.

Old Testament Background

The Old Testament has a major truth in Psalm 24:1: "The earth is the Lord's, and all it contains" (NASB). The familiar text succinctly states this premise: Creation gives way to accountability. In Everett Tilson's splendid chapter "Old Testament Background" in *Theological Perspectives of Stewardship*, he summarized his studies with these conclusions:

> 1. No part of man's life or world can be separated from the sphere of human stewardship, anymore than a part of man's life or world can be separated from the sphere of divine Lordship. 2. God freely yields creation into the hands of men in order that human beings, through their use of property, might bear witness to their divine destiny within the familyhood of man. . . . 7. God enacts his redemptive work in history through the gracious deeds of his faithful stewards.[6]

The Parables of Jesus

Perhaps the richest source of teaching in the Bible about stewardship is found in the parables of Jesus. He related the precepts to the ultimate meaning of life which closely parallels the major Old Testament conclusions.

In the parable of the talents (Matt. 25:14-30), Jesus spoke of a man going on a journey. Before his departure, the man called three trusted stewards and gave them instructions about managing his property while he was away. Two of the three made plans! They did long-range planning before they invested. They were successful and were amply rewarded. The one who planned the most was the one most amply and generously rewarded. One failed completely because he failed to plan. Some of the harshest words in the New Testament are directed to the one-talent steward whose lack of planning brought forth the ire of the owner.

The inevitability of judgment is associated with Jesus' dramatic words, "Now after a long time the master . . . came and settled accounts with them" (Matt. 25:19, NASB). Few parables stress planning more than this one. If stewardship means managing all of one's life, influence, and resources in light of an ultimate accounting, it is essential to stress planning. Jesus' emphasis on stewardship involved responsibility and responsible actions.

The center of Jesus' presentation of stewardship is that the steward (disciple) is responsible to the owner (God the Creator). This responsibility involves accountability. Witness both the parable of the talents and the parable of the dishonest steward (Luke 16:1-13). Although Jesus did not use the terms *stewardship* and *steward* often, the terms appear in both His parable of the dishonest steward and the wise and foolish servants (Luke 12:42-48).

The theme of responsible action emerges in many of Jesus' most forceful and familiar stories. We see it particularly in Luke's sequence of parables: the rich man and Lazarus (Luke 16:19-31), The rich fool (Luke 12:10-21), the unprofitable servant (Luke 17:7-10), the parable of the pounds (Luke 19:11-28). All these parables stress the inevitable and final accountability that humans in general, and Christians in particular, have but one response to the coming Kingdom in relation to the use of time, opportunity, and material possessions. They are stewards, either good ones or bad ones!

William R. Farmer's words are conclusive and forceful: "If you were to ask me what do the gospels of Matthew, Mark, Luke, and John teach about stewardship—I would have to say: *they teach us that we are to live our lives in response to what God accomplishes in us through Jesus Christ.*" Motivation for a minister's planning and discipline in personal financial management inevitably must return to this foundation.

Unbalanced priorities and resulting anxieties can erode this foundation.

On the other hand, some ministers sincerely object to financial planning because they consider it a breach of faith in the Almighty's order of things. "After all," they contend, "Jesus said, 'Take no thought for your life.' Remember the ravens and the lilies, and don't be concerned about things material." To cite this passage out of context is to misunderstand the mind of the Creator who planned and ordered His creation. Plants and animals indeed do live by the "laws of nature," but even a plant can "starve." The azaleas in my garden require food of a certain acid type, or they will not survive. Herds of wild animals die of starvation or freeze to death. Even the squirrels in my backyard stash away acorns (and my pecans!) for winter food.

Although the animal world exists by instinct, people live in a higher order, that of reason, which they are expected to use. Jesus had something much more profound in mind when He spoke of this "divinely careless" existence. Taken as a whole, Jesus' teachings in Matthew 6 and Luke 12 are teachings favoring a healthy perspective toward material things in order to alleviate anxiety. One's money does not have first priority, but neither should one "tempt the Lord thy God" by taking unnecessary risks for survival.

If Jesus' words are taken literally, then humans can be expected to function on little more than the animal or primitive level of instinct. Seeking first the kingdom of God and His righeousness places the spiritual life above the physical, but it does not deny a physical existence and the necessity of coping intelligently. A sense of stewardship promotes astute planning that can alleviate anxiety about material needs.

Let me encourage you to read and reread the basic parables on biblical stewardship. Whether one has a financial plan, these forceful stories can produce a conviction to act when one reads Jesus' words on responsible living. Christian stewardship is, indeed, the highest form of the responsible life.

Taken as a unit, these parables speak to the simple fact that, like it or not, all are stewards. We may be good stewards or bad stewards, but we are stewards, not mere instinctive creatures. The Christian, and above all the pastor, should deeply desire to be a good steward out of the ultimate motive of gratitude to God the Creator who has redeemed us in Jesus Christ, our Lord and Savior. This desire is related to the pastoral function, but even more important, it should be tied into the freedom of action and the joy of accomplishment when a personal, workable, and growing financial plan functions in good order.

Paul and Stewardship

One other source of biblical foundation on the principles of stewardship emerges from the unique, formative influence Paul had upon the early church. Out of Paul's Jewish background he continued with unusual strength in his conviction that the strongest incentive for stewardship rests fundamentally on the redemptive power of Christ, the cross, and the resurrection. Every choice that Paul made after the Damascus Road experience rested on the foundation that he had been "bought with a price" (1 Cor. 6:19-20). His most mature thinking about stewardship is found in 2 Corinthians 8—9. He encouraged the Corinthians to give to help the poorer Christians in Judea. His methods of encouraging the Corinthians to be generous and concerned about the offering are classic in their skillfulness and sensitivity, yet much more is involved. It coincides with a continuing theme throughout the Bible—our response in the right use of material things must grow out of a gratitude to God for His creation and redemption (2 Corinthians 8:9,13-14,24).

Paul would be right at home with the widespread emphasis today upon Christian life-styles, the contemporary emphasis that as Christians we should keep life as simple as possible so that we might give and share more to spread the message of Christ to the lost world. The emphasis on sharing united with Paul's constant concern that Gentile believers help the suffering Jewish believers. Ultimately, it comes back to his conviction that salvation was the free gift of God's grace, a gift which graciously lays upon every Christian the obligation of stewardship.[1] It would be inconceivable to Paul to separate salvation, sharing, and service. As one writer put it:

> Paul's life under the Cross as apostle and steward was lived in the context of a Christ-inaugurated new order of being, a revolutionary

"dispensation" of the spirit in which all who believed were "Sons of God." This fixed the Apostle's stewardship within the prior and greater stewardship of God, who had set it forth in his eternal plan of redemption.[8]

Planning and Stewardship

Planning is mandated as a response to these concepts of Christian stewardship. Not to plan invites tragedy. A pastor in a West Texas town had the sincere conviction that "the rapture of the church" would take place in his lifetime. This became a consuming conviction. It led to some unusual directions in his personal financial planning. His conviction was that theologically there was absolutely no need for long-range planning of personal finances. He carried no insurance; he refused to participate in Social Security; he resolutely ignored any denominational pension plan. Tragically, he died of a heart attack in his early forties, leaving a wife and several small children bereft. A neighboring pastor brought the family's dilemma to the attention of the denomination's relief assitance department. Some help was forthcoming, but at best it was inadequate. Planning ahead is sensible and indicative of faith in God.

Jesus' teaching on stewardship brings a basic balance and perspective. These grow out of the Old Testament background and are confirmed by Paul's powerful teaching. Life will end. There will be a time when the kingdom of God is consummated. Faith in God's providing power is essential. Yet, because individuals are responsible for managing their lives, influence, and resources, planning in the interval while existence is devloping is essential. All Christians are under the mandate of these solid and obvious biblical principles.

Of all people, pastors should be responsive to this fundamental logic. Many are. Today's seminarians hear these appeals in classes on church administration. They are responding as never before to the techniques of money management. The biblical foundations from the Old and New Testaments are in focus for a majority of the ministers in all age categories. The few horror stories of the short-sighted and misguided ones are giving way to many more balanced and concerned ministers who sincerely want assistance.

No one will dispute the conclusions that today's pastor has more material wealth than any other generation of ministers in history. Yet exceptions do occur. A deacon was serving on a pastor-search committee for a church whose pastor retired after a quarter of a century in that church. The committee came to the negotiating stage with a prospective minister. The deacon then learned that the prospective pastor's salary and allowances in a church somewhat smaller than theirs was exactly double what they had been paying. They raised the salary, but that deacon still is in a state of shock.

What many church officials refuse to accept is the real-dollar issue in ministers' salaries. What many pastors fail to apply is the biblical foundation of stewardship. Even ministers with high salaries can be victims of mismanagement. The same application holds for a rural pastor with a meager salary as for the super-church pastor with the highest salary in Christian history. The Christian, pastor and member alike, is mandated by biblical principles "to manage responsibly all of one's life, influence, and resources."

Notes

1. Lee E. Davis and Ernest D. Standerfer, *Christian Stewardship in Action* (Nashville: Convention Press, 1983), p. 5.

2. Cecil A. Ray, *How to Specialize in Christian Living* (Nashville: Convention press, 1982), p. 44.

3. Richard Cunningham, *Creative Stewardship* (Nashville: Abingdon Press, 1979), p. 35.

4. Everett Tilson, "Old Testament Background," *Theological Perspectives of Stewardship*, Edwin A. Briggs, ed. (Evanston, Ill.: The General Board of the Laity, United Methodist Church, 1969), p. 19.

5. A. R. Fagan, *What the Bible Says About Stewardship* (Nashville: Convention Press, 1976), p. 9.

6. Tilson, p.22.

7. William R. Farmer, "The New Testament Gospels," *Theological Perspectives of Stewardship*, Edwin A. Briggs, ed. (Evanston, Ill.: The General Board of the Laity, United Methodist Church, 1969), p. 39.

8. James H. Pyke, "Paul's Stewardship Mission" in Briggs, p. 60.

3

"Where Did All the Money Go?"
(Or the Essentials of Planning a Budget)

Several years ago, a noted television commentator on a popular news program pondered one evening, "Where did all the money go?" Like most people, he never used a budget. Now he was having a difficult time remembering where all the money he had earned since his discharge from the United States Army following World War II had gone. He believed his family had spent money wisely and carefully, but where?

He estimated that through the years he had spent almost $137,000 for food and beverages for his family of six. The home he purchased in 1951 for $29,500 cost him about $50,000 to maintain. Utilities during the time he lived there totaled $87,500. He estimated that he spent a total of $63,000 for transportation. Fuel costs for driving cars was the most difficult to determine because of the changes in gallon costs, especially during the oil crisis of the 1970s. He figured his expenditures for gasoline and oil were about $34,000.

College education for each of the man's four children totaled $96,000. For miscellaneous expenditures, such as clothing, hair cuts, appliances, and other, he figured his family spent some $200,000. His last expense was taxes which, after he computed his "guesstimate," reached the staggering total of $400,000. Collectively, the commentator estimated he had spent about $1.06 million. During the years since his discharge, he estimated he had earned some $1,250,000. "If I've earned $1.25 million and I've spent $1.06 million, what did I do with the other $190,000?"

Do You Know Where Your Money Goes?

Like the commentator, most people do not know where their money goes. And like millions of other Americans, they fret and wonder how they are going to make their incomes at least match their expenses. Not one minister in ten thousand makes the money the commentator did, but most ministers ask the same question: Where did all the money go?

Money is nothing more than a tool with which to obtain what one needs and wants. How effectively one controls money is the key to a successful plan. Money management requires planning that avoids the pitfalls of waste and grabs the wise opportunities. Developing a functional plan requires time. A person cannot expect new efforts to produce complete financial independence overnight after spending years of neglecting to maintain budget control.

Financial planning is neither complicated nor mysterious. Setting up a personal financial plan does pose a problem for many because they do not know where to start.

This chapter is designed to unravel the problem and thereby eliminate the frustrations that you and your family experience with today's finances. You will find ways to break your financial resources and needs into small units. If you follow the step-by-step procedure, you will organize them into an intelligent program of spending, saving, giving, and investing priorities. Once you complete your plan, your family's budget will be your own and may be radically different from others you may know. What you allocate in your budget will depend upon your personal goals and priorities. You will know what money is coming in each month and from what sources and what funds you must set aside for bills and for your future needs and security. You will also know exactly how much money you have left to meet the day-to-day expenses for items such as food, clothing, housing, and transportation.

Make Financial Planning a Family Matter

Before anything is put on paper, you must first pick a manager to keep the records of the family's spending and saving. If you are single, you are elected to keep your own budget. If you are married, you and your spouse must decide. Once a month (or at least once a quarter), the family should gather to discuss its financial position. If you have children, involve them in your discussions and planning.

Making the financial plan a family project will be one of the soundest decisions you can make. Some books on financial management specifically recommend the wife keep the books because usually she outlives her husband; furthermore, she may have more day-to-day contact with costs if she goes to the supermarket and also buys the families clothes.

First Steps in Budgeting

Nothing is really complicated about financial planning. Creating and developing your financial plan is easy when you know your net worth and relate it to your personal financial budget. To do this, follow these five steps.

1. Set goals and develop financial priorities based upon your family's ultimate goals, including retirement.
2. Determine your present financial status.
3. Figure your current expenses.
4. Set up records for maintaining and controlling expenditures.
5. Review and evaluate your plan, and modify it as needed.

As you begin to develop information pertaining to each of the five steps, keep in mind that no two families, not even two people, have the same financial needs. Recall the five ministers in the first chapter and their variety of needs.

Develop Financial Priorities

Using the first steps in budgeting, the first element is to know what your family wants to accomplish in its financial plan. Establish your goals step by step until you are where you want to be. Take a moment to dream big. By thinking and planning, you come to grips with questions such as, Where am I now? and Where do I want to be in ninety days, one year, five years, ten years, and twenty years? Be as specific as possible as you focus on the things you want to accomplish. For example, the long-range goal of every minister should be to have a debt-free home and an ample retirement fund. Another long-range goal may be to have enough money to take a trip to some distant land. Again, think big!

Your intermediate goals are those you want to reach in one to ten years. Maybe your desire is to pay college costs. Perhaps you want a new car or need to make some major repair to your home.

Finally, determine your immediate or short-range goals. These are goals you can reach in sixty days to one year, and they might include reducing your debt, buying new insurance poilicies or new furniture.

Once you have determined your goals, record them in the front of your family's financial budget book. Compare them periodically with what actually has happened. Never hesitate to adjust your goals whenever it is appropriate.

Use the spaces below to list your family's goals.

Long-Range Goals
(20 Years to Retirement)

_____

_____

_____

_____

Intermediate Goals
(1 Year to 10 Years)

_____

_____

_____

_____

Immediate Goals
(60 Days to 1 Year)

_____

_____

_____

_____

_____

_____

Determine Your Financial Status

To determine your financial status, begin by totaling every dollar of income your family expects to receive for spending during the year. If you and your spouse work, include both of your earnings. List only the actual net take-home pay (after all deductions have been made for income taxes, Social Security, group insurance, retirement plan, and any other item that is withheld regularly).

To this, add all the income you expect to receive from interest on bonds, savings, bonuses, stock dividends, tax refunds, property rentals, and miscellaneous sources such as weddings, funerals, speaking engagements, and revivals. Also give an accounting of income from any profits or monies you receive from the sale of real estate, home, automobile, stocks, bonds, or other securities.

If you earn money on an irregular basis from sources such as sales or writing, record these also. Remember, your income inventory must reflect actual amounts, not estimates. When your income increases because of raises or extra effort, adjust your financial plan. Likewise, if your income decreases, adjust your plan.

The following work sheet will guide you in computing your total income. When it is completed, file it in your family's financial budget book.

Our Family Income for 19

INCOME

Salaries (Net amounts)

You . . . .$_____

Your spouse . . . . _____

Bonus(es) . . . . _____

Loan(s) . . . . _____

Other . . . . _____

TOTAL SALARIES $_____

Investment Income

Interest (Taxable) . . . .$_____

Interest (nontaxable) . . . . _____

Dividends . . . . _____

Real Estate . . . . _____

Profit Sharing . . . . _____

TOTAL INVESTMENT INCOME $_____

Other Income

Cash Gifts . . . .$_____

Bonus(es) . . . . _____

Inheritance . . . . _____

Other . . . . _____

TOTAL OTHER INCOME $_____

NET INCOME FOR 12 MONTHS

OF 19

Net income is the amount available for spending on everything during the year. Does the total surprise you?

Because most bills are due and payable each month, you need to know your total monthly income, so divide *Net Income* by twelve.

Figure Your Expenses/Set Up Records

Knowing how much money you have is important, but more important is knowing how it is being spent. If you have kept records of any kind, such as receipts for puchases, check stubs, or bills of sale, they will make establishing a plan easier. You can purchase record-keeping forms, but it is better if you tailor them to fit your own needs from the ones used in these pages.

For simplification, all expenditures will be broken down into fixed or variable categories. The following list classifies most budget items.

Fixed expenses are those that must be paid regularly and regarded as already spent. These include:

    Tithe and love offerings to your church

    Housing costs (rent or home mortgage payments)

    Utilities such as electricity, gas, water, telephone, garbage collection, sewage, and fuel

    All premiums for life, medical, dental, home, and auto insurance

    Membership dues in professional organizations and clubs

    Installment loans

    Federal and state income taxes and Social Security taxes

    Personal allowances

    Subscriptions to papers and magazines

Variable expenses are those that can be decreased, increased, or omitted. Itemize these from your statements, receipts, or check stubs. If you have not kept them, you can either estimate the amounts or determine how much you spend by keeping records for one or two months on these items. Variable expenses include:

    Home improvements and maintenance

    Clothing and laundry

    Household furnishings, repairs, and renovations

    Personal care, such as barber, beauty shop

    Entertainment, such as theater, hobbies, parties, sports

    Recreation and vacations

    Gifts for birthdays, weddings, anniversaries, graduation

    Transportation, such as bus, train or plane, fuel, car repairs, and auto insurance.

    Miscellaneous: all things not listed

From these categories, you can create your budget using the sample work sheets.

Fixed Expenses Work Sheet
These are items we must pay each month.

Items	Jan	Feb	Mar	Quarter
CHURCH Tithe and Offering				
HOUSING Mortgage or Rent				
UTILITIES Lights				
Gas or Fuel				
Water				
Telephone				
Other				
INSURANCE Life				
Medical				
Accident				
Home				
Auto				
Other				
INSTALLMENT LOANS				
TAXES Income				
Personal				
Real Estate				
Social Security				
SAVINGS Emergency Fund				
OTHER				
Total Amount for Fixed Expenses				

Variable Expenses Work Sheet
These are items we must pay each month.

Items	Jan	Feb	Mar	Quarter
FOOD AND BEVERAGES				
CLOTHING				
TRANSPORTATION Auto				
Bus				
Other				
MEDICAL AND DENTAL				
HOUSEHOLD EXPENSES Furniture				
Maintenance				
Equipment				
EDUCATION				
GIFTS AND DONATIONS Church				
Fund Raising				
Other				
INSTALLMENTS Credit Cards				
Other				
RECREATION				
MISCELLANEOUS				
OTHER				
Total Amount for Variable Expenses				

FAMILY FINANCIAL RECORD

_____ MONTH   _____ YEAR

	TITHE AND GIFTS	FOOD IN AND OUT	HOUSING UTILITY	TRANSPOR-TATION	MEDICAL CARE
Amount to Spend	$	$	$	$	$
Day 1					
2					
3					
4					
5					
6					
7					
8					
9					
10					
11					
12					
13					
14					
15					
16					
17					
18					
19					
20					
21					
22					
23					
24					
25					
26					
27					
28					
29					
30					
31					
TOTAL					

Monthly Recap

Net Income to Spend
Salary(ies) $_____
Interest $_____
Other $_____
TOTAL INCOME $_____   TOTAL EXPENSES $_____

FAMILY FINANCIAL RECORD

_____   _____
MONTH   YEAR

CLOTHING	PERSONAL CARE	SAVINGS	ENTERTAIN-MENT	MISCELLANEOUS
$_____	$_____	$_____	$_____	$_____

Special Notes on New Budget Items

_____
_____
_____

Review and Evaluate

The ideal budget is one in which your income regularly exceeds your expenses. Ideally, your income is greater than your expenses. If this is not true, review your work sheets and adjust your budget. If you still cannot make your income exceed your expenses, a family financial record can be very important for you. With it you will be able to determine where and when your money is being spent. For at least thirty days, keep a detailed accounting of where your money is going. At the end of the accounting period, evaluate once again. If your spending is too far out of line, can you determine the reason? Here is where your family must keep working and reworking the budget until income equals or exceeds spending.

Once more, the key to successful personal money management is disciplined planning. As your family circumstances change, you will find yourself adjusting and reorganizing your plan to fit your new goals.

Conclusion

For a budget plan to work, you need to know where the money goes. You can know. You must know. This is true whether you are like David S. at the outset of your ministry or like Clyde C. You must know enough about the things you buy to make certain you are getting your money's worth. You must make sensible decisions about what you will and will not buy. The end result is to balance expenses and income, all within the guidelines that you and your family have chosen.

In budgeting, forget the get-rich-quick schemes. Ignore the barrage of flyers about instant wealth. Most ministers will always have a moderate income. With good planning, you can use moderate, sometimes minimum, income to attain your goals. It takes care, common sense, Christian stewardship, and understanding your limitations to manage your money. It is never too late to begin. Though it may be difficult to change your habits, it can be done.

Please do not fall into the trap of thinking all of your problems will be solved if you can earn more money. A salary raise or a second income through your wife's job may be welcomed, but the underlying premise still holds: You can and you must manage what you have. Begin with a budget!

4

Taking Complete Charge of Finances

Now that you have put on paper where your money comes from and where it goes, you have a good overview of where your family stands. The ideal situation is to have more income than expenses.

Beginning now, you really take charge of your financial plan development. The first thing to remember about financial planning is that "what was valid for yesterday may not be so today, and by tomorrow, it will be different." Your needs will change. You can count on it! Tax laws change, and inflation rates fluctuate. Hence, the only way to protect the value of your estate is to update your plan.

This kind of planning produces ways of reducing taxes as much as possible. With the Federal Economic Recovery Tax Act of 1981 and the tax laws passed in 1984, radical changes were made that reduced tax liabilities for about 96 percent of the estates in the United States. Now the emphasis is to arrange your planning so that all your properties will be transmitted to the people and institutions of your choice.

Real financial planning means starting as soon as you can, keeping your debts under control, and saving for the future.

In recent years, individuals have begun to seek professional estate planning advice. In the business community, many companies provide extensive counseling for employees, as well as seminars and training on financial and estate planning, health maintenance, and ways to deal with leisure time.

Many denominations today hold seminars and offer printed materials about financial and estate planning. Do not become confused with the terms *financial planning* and *estate planning*. Consider the two in this manner: Financial planning is every aspect of accounting and the use of the family's income, estate planning concentrates on future benefits provided by wills, trusts, gifts, and life insurance. Simplified even more, financial planning is making basic choices about spending and saving your income; estate planning means deciding who is to have what you have earned or have acquired.

This book is designed to help you pull together vital information, then show you how to focus on your needs. You may begin to feel inadequate in certain areas of your planning, especially estate development. Realize that no one can be an expert in everything, but do seek competent professional consultants.

Use Professional Consultants when Needed

An attorney will help you understand the laws of your state and how to plan with these laws in mind. A lawyer will also assist you with other legal aspects of financial planning, such as applications for federal and state estate taxes, and preparation of legal documents, such as wills and trusts.

A life underwriter, working with other advisors, will help you select the right kind of insurance to meet your needs. An underwriter can also show you how to reduce taxes and other expenses related to your estate.

An accountant will help you prepare your financial statements and tax returns. He will also assist in valuing your properties.

A trust officer can advise you about investments and property management.

Another source of help is the continuous flow of books and articles on money management. Though most of these publications are not written from the minister's point of view, many have excellent and relevant ideas. A minister who has studied many biblical commentaries knows how to select applicable ideas. The same works in the financial field of resources. Use your public library for these materials. Take notes from them. Realize how quickly some of these materials become obsolete. Included in Suggested Resources are a number of titles which have helped me; perhaps they will assist you as well.

How to Use Credit

Using cash is the most economical way to purchase today. A few American families pay cash for everything, but the majority have been or will be in debt because they are unable to pay cash for items they consider necessary. Debt is not bad when it is used correctly. Many young couples would be unable to establish a household or have children without the use of credit. Families that are successful in using credit will plan purchases which fit into their family budgets. Credit today is providing many families with goods often considered as luxury items. An example is the automobile. Without the opportunity to purchase cars on installment loans, our problems would be compounded. Debt for automobiles, then, is a necessity for most of us.

Debt can also be a devastating foe. The ability to buy on "easy terms" plus the availability of those plastic cards have carried far too many families into financial chaos. Debt can become the main cause of stress on the family. People may suffer mental anxiety worrying about going into bankruptcy or losing their jobs when they cannot make payments. Money mismanagement, as every minister has witnessed among his people, can lead to marital breakdowns. Approximately one out of three marriages today ends in divorce, and poor money management is one of the leading causes.

Is there a way to determine how to use credit wisely? Is there a way to determine what a family's debt limitations should be?

My pastor friend who gave the sage advice to couples beginning their ministry added another gem. He learned how to make credit work for him and his family, especially when inflation is rampant. "Use credit as a tool for making the best use of your money," he said. He recalled during the late 1970s that his refrigerator stopped running and could not be repaired. He and his wife had saved some money, but it was not enough to buy a new one. They purchased a new one with a national bank credit card and spread the payments over four months.

They bought the refrigerator at the right time. Inflation had forced the price up almost $90 over the original price before they made their final payment. The finance charges for the four months was just under $15. By using credit wisely, they were able to use the refrigerator while paying for it. More important, they saved almost $75.

Being able to use credit is a privilege. The advantages of buying on credit are available to everyone who keeps buying under control. Most people usually can afford to allocate up to 15 percent of their take-home pay to installment debt, not including home mortgage payments. When more than 15 percent is needed, it is difficult to make ends meet. Let us assume your take-home pay after taxes is $20,000. Reduce this amount by your mortgage (assume 25 percent). If you are living in a church parsonage, set aside a fixed amount toward the purchase of your own home. (More will be said about this in chapter 7.) After deducting the mortgage, the remainder amounts to $15,000 to cover everything your family needs. Your debt ceiling under this plan is $2,250 a year.

Another approach, more conservative and safer, is to limit debt to 10 percent of your take-home pay. Using the example of a $20,000 income, the maximum ceiling is $2,000 for a twelve-month period. Before entering into any indebtedness, determine the maximum amount of credit your family can safely handle and abide by it. The way you handle indebtedness in your personal life will make a definite impression on the people to whom you are ministering and witnessing.

Choosing the Right Credit

If you have a record of paying bills regularly, you can obtain credit easily. It is not unusual to be sent credit cards in the mail. And when you walk in department stores and banks, you are bombarded by ways to obtain easy credit. All you have to do is complete the short application. Truly we are in the plastic credit period.

Should you use credit cards? Only you can answer that, but generally you should if you can treat each charge purchase as if you were paying cash. Always ask yourself, Can I repay this on time and without great financial burden? If you decide to apply for cards, select only those you need and will use regularly, such as a bank charge card, an oil company card, and perhaps a major department store card. You may want to consider one of the travel entertainment cards, such as American Express, for the business part of your ministry.

Numerous other types of charge accounts and debt loans are available, ranging from the department store open thirty-day account to installment loans and long-term loans offered by banks and financial institutions to the small loan company that specializes in personal and automobile loans and will take more high-risk creditors than other similar agencies.

When making a purchase or borrowing money, ask the seller or lender to define the terms used. Significant differences can occur in the way the small print of the sales agreement or contract reads. Know what you are committing to before you sign on the line. Once you sign your name, you are obligated for everything in the agreement.

Shop Around for Credit Rates

Good shoppers are always looking for bargains. Yet, far too many people will take the first offer of credit without comparing prices. Few realize they have a choice. They are usually more concerned with the amount of the monthly payment. If it appears to be low enough to fit into their spending plan, they are satisfied. As a consumer, you are truly in the driver's seat today. The Truth-in-Lending Law requires that full disclosure be given about all interest rates. This information includes the amount of the loan subject to interest, the daily rate of interest, and the corresponding annualized percentage rate. Sometimes interest rates and their computations are presented in narrative rather than statistical form, making it difficult to decipher. In addition to legally stated, hard-to-understand explanations, many merchants use different methods for applying interest rates. Some place all costs under the term *finance charge* which can be the total of all charges they require before you can obtain credit.

The best practice is to ask how much you will be charged and what it represents. Once you know the finance charge and the annual percentage rate, you then know how much you are paying to borrow money or buy on credit.

How to Compute Interest

You can compute the percentage of interest charged by using this simple formula:

$$\frac{2\,m\,I}{P(n+1)} = RI$$

Here is how it works. Suppose you purchase an item for $100 at a cost of $10, payable in 12 monthly payments. Your true rate of interest will be 18.46 percent.

RI = annual percentage charge
m = 12 (number of payments per year)
I = $10
P = $100 (net amount of loan)
n = 12 (total payments made)

$$\frac{2(12)\,10}{\$100\,(12+1)} = 18.46\%$$

Usually simple interest is the least expensive and easiest to compute. The same $100 in the example above with a $10 interest charge payable in one payment at the end of 12 months will cost you only 10 percent. Before you borrow, know what you will be paying.

Examples of Interest on Unpaid Balance

When you are charged monthly on the unpaid balance, you may be paying a high rate of interest. Here are typical charges you may find on your statements:

Cost Per Month	Annual Interest Rate
$3/4$%	9%
1	10
$1^{1}/_{2}$	18
2	24
$2^{1}/_{2}$	30
3	36
$3^{1}/_{2}$	42

What to Do if You Cannot Pay

It is terrifying to think you might not be able to pay your debts. This does happen, however, even to ministers of the gospel. When it does, do not panic, but do not think the problem will go away. Your debts are legal obligations that must be handled to completion to maintain your good name. The merchant, bank, or store does not want to create problems for you. All it wants is its money. If you ever find yourself unable to make a payment, act immediately. Call the credit manager of the store and explain your predicament. Usually at this point, something can be worked out that is agreeable to all. But do something positive before your name becomes tainted with a bad credit risk.

Keeping your credit rating in good stead is very important. Poor handling can result in years of embarrassment. Pastor search committees nearly always run a credit check on prospective pastors. It is awkward when interest in an individual wanes because of poor financial management reports.

Tips on Cutting Expenses

Awareness of some common reasons for spending will assist in keeping of budget in line and in actually enjoying the adventure of good financial management. Consider these suggestions:

Curb Your Impulsive Buying

Prepare yourself when you go to the grocery store. These places are notorious for putting displays at the proper places for maximum temptation. Prepare your shopping list in advance and stick to it. If other members of your family accompany you, educate them in advance about the negative impact of impulsive buying.

Family members are also enticed at other stores such as the book store, the clothing store, or recreation outlets. The list is long. The need to curb impulses is great. This is a good place for me to confess my addiction to impulsive buying. We handle some of it in our family by my wife's doing the grocery shopping *alone!*

Shop Around for Sales and Specials

Since food and clothing constitute a high percentage of the family budget, it makes sense to be aware of seasonal sales, weekly specials at the supermarket, and other values, such as coupons, and garage sales.

Monitor Automobile Costs Carefully

"Blessed are ye when a church provides a car for the pastor." The ideal arrangement for the minister seems to be a church-owned car with operating costs paid. Many churches provide a car because of the constant use a minister makes of it in the direct work of the pastorate. Many more churches do not make this provision. Some give adequate allowances; many, again, do not.

In most ministers' budgets, a lot of money is spent unsuspectingly for high automobile operating costs. If you have the responsibility of purchasing the car, check carefully into your options. Since there are a thousand and one of them, these brief paragraphs can only call attention to monitoring the costs.

Make your church aware of the business expense of this necessary phase of the ministry. Do not buy unnecessary equipment. Learn to make some simple repairs and replacements such as an oil change and spark plugs. Locate and use a discount auto parts store.

One minister thought it was beneath his dignity to crawl under his car and change the oil filter. Then came the day when it had to be done, and he realized his budget would not permit the usual trip to the service station. Armed with resolve and a little money, he bought the filter and oil at one third of what he usually paid. When the task was finished in less than an hour, he marveled at the satisfaction he experienced both in savings and in doing something which turned out less distasteful than he imagined.

Remember the absolute importance of complete and accurate records in the operation, purchase, and depreciation of your automobile. All of this is relevant to some excellent opportunities for a major income tax deduction. A business deducation can be taken in one of two ways. The simplest way is to deduct from your taxable income a certain amount per mile for the first fifteen thousand miles used for business. This is called the standard deduction.

The second option is to itemize all costs of operating your car. This includes all variable costs, such as fuel, oil, tires, repairs, and maintenance, plus all fixed costs, such as insurance, registration, and depreciation.

Time Your Major Purchases

Clothing is a major expense for most families. Avoid buying during the Easter and Christmas seasons, but go to the after-Christmas sale, the midsummer sale, and the discount store. Discipline yourself to shopping for the off season sales. Time the buying of your new car when the new models come out, but make it last year's model! You will be surprised at the savings. Timing can give you a 50 percent saving on certain major expenditures, such as furniture and appliances. School yourself accordingly. Watch for deceptive advertising. Rarely ever yield to phone solicitation. A basic rule is to put yourself in the driver's seat when it comes to spending your money.

Maintain a Regular Savings Strategy

The average American family saves less than 4 percent of its income. Many advisors recommend a minimum of 10 percent. The sad fact remains that many American families, including many ministers, have no savings. Regular saving is essential if you are to be in charge of your finances. Savings will help when emergencies arise, and saving will encourage the fulfillment of your goals.

Maintin some systematic saving plan, even if it is a minimal amount. Consider it as paying yourself out of your check. Put your loose change in a savings account. One pastor's wife worked out an arrangement with her husband whereby all the loose change they had at the end of each day would be collected in a "vacation fund." When she had enough for a nonembarrassing deposit at a local savings and loan company, she put the money in the account. Occasionally, they added other money, especially honorariums from weddings and other pastoral services. Instead of being used as a vacation fund, it grew enough to be used to pay educational expenses for the children.

Your savings account can be at a bank, a credit union, a savings and loan institution, or money can be put in U. S. government bonds. The family needs to agree on its use—an emergency fund, college fund, or down payment on a car. Accumulate an amount equal to six months of your salary in this fund.

Conclusion

The main thrust of this chapter has been to challenge you to take control rather than to be buffeted by the constant pressure of finances. Two steps have been stressed: (1) Take charge of your finances through planning; (2) spend wisely and save. There is no substitute for planning, and no one can do it for you. Many resources are available to help you plan, but the initiative is up to you and your family. It is worth all the effort.

If you have followed the recommendations outlined so far, you have completed the first phase in establishing a management system for your family's finances. To get to this point, your family will have thought about the spending of your income and the alternatives for doing a more effective job. You may need to cut back expenditures and edit carefully to reach the goals you established for your immediate objectives. This will be especially true if you want to reduce your debt.

Now you will soon be ready to consider some further goals.

5

Insurance and Long-Term Goals

Several reminders are in order before you consider long-range insurance goals. First, wise goals are both flexible and variable. Second, itemize your compensation package before setting goals. And third, think taxes always.

Variables in Goal Setting

Variables abound in goal setting. As you experiment with them, you will focus on the ones that will benefit you. Also, remember that your goals can be altered and changed as the ages and size of your family change. Any change in your income will affect your goals. Adjust your goals to meet new challenges. Compare your projected goals with what occurs monthly, quarterly, and annually. Allocating money effectively is exciting!

Itemize Your Compensation Package

Financial goal planning covers the entire spectrum of family money management, including designated allowances. The total compensation provided by churches usually includes more than take-home pay. Often the church lumps together such items as housing allowances, automobile allowances, retirement and insurance programs, library or book allowances, and convention expenses. Yet it is important that the funds for each of these categories be segregated in the budget of your church. When allowances for performing your duties as a pastor are incorporated into your salary, it can lead to misunderstandings within the congregation. Your cash salary and your housing allowance should be the only items listed under "Salary." Your congregation should know the amount of your salary and the various allowances. Segregating your compensation makes your family budget keeping easier, especially when prepaying your income tax.

Think Taxes Year Around

Another consideration is taxes. Like the majority of taxpayers, the minister, except for the filing of his quarterly return, usually views income taxes as a one-time-a-year problem. However, it is both wise and necessary to adopt "Think Tax" as a motto anytime money enters or leaves your hands.

Does income tax confuse you? The Internal Revenue Service and a large number of private organizations are helpful sources for tax help year around. Look in your daily papers and news magazines for articles on taxes. Congress and the courts frequently change or modify tax laws. For you to be less than fully aware of the different methods and aids to reduce your taxes is to be remiss in your responsibility to yourself and your family. Being aware of tax law changes early also enables you to rearrange your financial affairs and reduce your income taxes. Taxes may be deferred, reduced, or spread. Existing laws can give you a substantial financial boost.

If you have not been using tax deferment, you may wonder: Is it worth the trouble? Would it be easier to pay the tax and avoid the red tape associated with tax deferment or tax shelters? When you postpone payment of taxes, you will have money in hand to earn additional revenue—another way to save money.

Develop Long-Range Goals

From this point onward, I will focus on the challenging aspects of long-range planning. Your strategy will be guided by your own personal criteria, such as your age, family size, and income. Look into the future and take legal and moral steps to assure that your family and beneficiaries will receive the benefits from your estate that you want them to have. Your plan should incorporate a way for your family to continue as a unit if you die before you have time to accumulate an estate. One quick way, however, to build an immediate estate is through *insurance*.

Everyone needs insurance, but how much and what kind? You will want to consider medical, disability, and, of course, life insurance. The simplest way to determine your personal insurance needs is to use the work sheets that follow. First, determine your current assets.

My Family Assets

Source	Amounts
Checking Accounts	$_____
Savings Accounts	_____
Denominational Pension Program Benefits	
Insurance	_____
Death Benefit(s)	_____
Life Insurance	_____
Stocks	_____
Bonds	_____
Mutual Funds	_____
Other Income	_____
	_____
Total Assets in Estate	$_____

The total asset picture for most ministers is usually far from adequate. In such cases, there is no substitute for insurance. In financial planning, income security is the great attraction of insurance. The Family Needs Work Sheet will show you how insurance can play a significant role in keeping your family financially secure.

Family Needs Work Sheet

Step	Item	Amount
1.	Current Total Annual Income	$_____
2.	Estimate of Family Income Needed (Approximately 75% of line 1)	_____
3.	Amount of Money Needed for:	
	Final Expenses (Include taxes)	_____
	Home Mortgage	_____

      Education of Children   _____

      Other Debts   _____

4. Estimate of Annual Income Available from
   Social Security
   (Include all benefits for children under
   age 18)   _____

5. Denominational Retirement Benefit Plan
   (Widow and/or Death Benefit)   _____

6. Other Income from:
   Veterans Benefits   _____
   Trust Funds   _____
   Personal Income   _____

7. Spouse's Income   _____

8. Total Anticipated Income Payable to Your
   Family (Add lines 3 through 7)   _____

9. Additional Income Needed Each Year by
   Your Family (Subtract line 8 from line 2)   _____

The major purpose of life insurance is to give your family financial protection that bridges the gap between the assets you now own and those required on line 9 when you die. Your net worth, expenses, income, family needs, and indebtedness must be considered in determining how much insurance you need. Insurance experts recommend, as a general rule, about five times annual salary as the minimum.

This amount will be inadequate if you are young and have small children. For example, David and Mary strive to make his $23,500 annual salary stretch. David's ultimate goal is to have sufficient protection to replace 75 percent of his current income. (This should be the goal of every minister, with 60 percent being the absolute minimum.) Since David's church pays the premium on his life insurance through the denominational pension board, the protection his dependents need is provided. David will need approximately $152,750 to insure that Mary receives 75 percent of his salary. To figure this, assume the benefit is invested at 5 percent and that Mary will convert the principal so that at her actuarial death nothing will remain. It is ironic that the younger a minister is, the less his insurance will cost, but it is during this period that he finds it most difficult to purchase.

Likewise, it takes more money to provide sufficent coverage for an older minister, such as forty-five-year-old Dr. Jones whose wife is also forty-five years old. On a $36,000 a year salary, Dr. Jones, to assure his wife 75 percent of his salary, needs insurance of $295,200. This amount does not include any income from savings, Social Security, or other types of insurance or investments.

Categories of Insurance

Although life insurance may be purchased in many different forms, every policy falls under one of two categories: term insurance and cash value insurance.

Regardless of the kind of insurance you buy or by what name it is called, the rates are computed on the assumption of death and are reflected in a mortality table. The true cost of life insurance rises each year as the likelihood of death increases.

Term insurance protects your life for a limited time at a low cost. When the contract expires, you have nothing, although you can usually renew term life at a higher rate. Term life usually is renewed every five years, although you can purchase one-, ten-, or twenty-year insurance until age sixty-five. Term insurance can be bought at a fixed level or at a decreasing amount.

Cash value insurance combines protection with a savings account that increases slowly in value each year. The face value remains the same, and the premium remains fixed. It can be combined with term insurance, and it pays about what you would earn on a passbook savings account on the cash reserve part. Cash value insurance is referred to as straight life, whole life, or ordinary life.

In recent years, many insurance companies have advertised a plan called by various names such as Universal Life, Variable Life, and Adjustable Life. This plan gives flexibility in death benefits and in premium. You can raise or lower your premium; you can raise or lower the amount of your coverage. It also allows you to use cash value and term insurance protection within the same policy.

What Kind of Insurance Should I Buy?

The first insurance coverage you should obtain is available through your denomination. This is the first place to look because:

1. Your denomination may provide a group program at a lower rate than if you purchased it yourself.

2. Your denominational plan is usually portable. This means you can continue your coverage as you move from one church to another.

3. Your denominational plan can usually be continued whether you serve a church or agency or whether you are a student or a full-time church or denominational worker.

Once you have obtained coverage through your denominational program, take a close look at additional term insurance. Your denomination may be able to help you with the program you need. Your local insurance agent also can help you with additional protection.

Income While Disabled

It has been projected that almost 30 percent of the population thirty years of age and over will be disabled for some length of time before they are sixty-five! If you are disabled, will you family have financial security? Do you have disability income insurance? Do you know how much Social Security will pay if you become disabled?

If you become disabled anytime before retirement, you will need at least 80 percent of your current income to continue living in your present style. Do you have that much available from any of the sources in the following work sheet?

Income for Disability

Source	Amount
Disability Benefits from	
Denominational Plan	$_____
Disability Insurance	_____
Interest and Dividends	_____
Trust Funds	_____
Other Income	_____
Social Security	_____
Total Income Available	
if I Become Disabled	$_____
Spouse's Income	$_____
Total	$_____

If your spouse's salary accounts for a substantial portion of your family's total income, the possibility of her becoming disabled should also be considered in your plan.

If the total above is inadequate, consult your denominational pension agency about the disability protection it provides. Contact your insurance agent and ask for a recommendation. He will evaluate your needs and make recommendations to fit your financial goals. Disability insurance usually will pay as much as 60 percent of your gross earnings.

Medical Insurance Program

In recent years the cost of health care has risen faster than inflation and has surpassed any other type of personal expense for products and services. In the majority of homes, the high cost is a major economic factor in the family budget. As a nation, Americans are spending more that $325 billion a year on health care. The majority of medical costs are earmarked for hospital care where the daily room rate can exceed $200. As people grow older, their anxieties center on the need for adequate medical insurance protection. That was Clyde's major concern when he resigned at age seventy-four because of health problems.

A family may have insurance for medical and hospital use in two principle ways. The group plan is the more common since more than 70 percent of all employers, denominational and secular, provide coverage and usually pay all or part of the premium. The second way is through an individual policy. Medical insurance programs through group arrangements usually are more economical than when purchased in individual packages.

If you have no denominational agency, by all means contact your insurance representative. When you obtain coverage individually, you can decide which medical needs to cover at specific periods. For example, if your family is at childbearing age, you will need maternity benefits. As your family grows older, you can change your coverage to meet your family's needs.

Medical insurance packages include part or all of the following benefits under a group, an individual, or a family plan.

Hospital—Benefits pay for services rendered in a hospital, such as room and board and routine nursing care. Many policies provide for outpatient services also.

Surgical—Benefits pay for the cost of surgical services, usually on a maximum basis for different sugical operations.

Physician—Benefits usually pay for a specific number of visits during an in-hospital stay and, in most cases, are combined with hospital and surgical benefits.

Major Medical—Benefits usually pay a percentage of the medical bill after you satisfy a deductible. Benefits pay for practically all types of medical care whether they are provided in or outside the hospital, with maximums up to $1,000,000.

Although most American families are protected by medical insurance, many of them do not know what they have. Review your insurance policy to understand the coverage in force and to decide if the amounts are enough to meet today's medical demands.

Few bargains exist in medical insurance today. Costs continue to rise while benefits decrease. The trend is toward a catastrophic concept of coverage. New plans, such as the Health Maintenance

Organization (HMO), are providing more coverage. Look at all types of plans before you spend your money.

Remember, the time to obtain insurance coverage is when you do not need it. Once you are on the way to the hospital or to the doctor with a major problem, it is too late!

Benefits Under Social Security

Social Security benefits are very important, but they usually are not sufficient to support retired persons with both the dignity and the comfort they need. The extra income from Social Security can also be important to your beneficiaries. You can obtain estimates on death and disability benefits for you and your family by contacting the Social Security Administration.

Social Security and the New Minister

As a new minister of the gospel, you have a stake in Social Security. Ministers have participated in this mammoth American social system on a self-employed basis since 1956. A few ministers do not participate because they sought exemption and received it under a single exception open only to clergy during the beginning of their ministries. The exemption applies only to income a minister receives as a member of the clergy; and once it has been approved, it cannot be revoked.

The exemption requires a soul-searching reply that cannot be taken lightly. Like every young minister, David S., the seminary graduate, had to make a choice. A month after he graduated from the seminary in May, his home church ordained him a minister of the gospel. David contacted his local Social Security office to discuss the direction he should take. He was shown Form 4361 and told that signing it would exempt him and his dependents from Social Security coverage and from paying the self-employment tax from ministerial services. David was impressed until he read somewhere that signing the form meant that, because of his religious principles, he was conscientiously opposed to accepting, for services performed as a member of the clergy, any public (governmental) insurance that makes payments in the event of death, disability, old age, or retirement. This included public insurance that makes payments toward the cost of, or provides services for, medical care including the benefits of any insurance system established by the Social Security Act.

This meant the exemption, if David accepted it, would eliminate him from all government benefits when he became disabled, died, or retired. He was unable to say he was totally against all government systems of social insurance.

David said he could oppose Social Security on the grounds that he did not want to pay for it, but economics is not an acceptable excuse for exemption.

The Internal Revenue Service (IRS) also maintains that the election is not valid if the exemption is for any reason other than that of conscience. The IRS can ask for definite religious reasons from any minister who files the exemption. If the answer is inadequate, IRS may declare it invalid, and the minister will be required to pay three years of self-employment taxes, interest on those taxes, and, in some cases, a negligence penalty.

If David could have conscientiously applied for exemption, he would have had to file Form 4361 by the date his income tax return was due, including all extensions, for the second tax year in which he had at least $400 in self-employment earnings. Once the deadline passes, no minister participating in Social Security may choose to stop participating in the plan.

David will begin filing Schedule SE (Form 1040) when he files his income tax on April 15.

In 1983, legislation was enacted that dramatically affected churches and church personnel. One provision called for all churches to include all employees in Social Security, something that had been optional before. Another amendment, raising the self-employment tax and salary base to record highs, directly affected the ordained minister who under Social Security is classified as self-employed.

In 1984, this rule was altered again, giving churches as employers some additional options. Since Congress meets annually and tinkers constantly with these important rules, please check with your local Social Security office or your denominational church pension board for the latest interpretations on these issues.

Note the tax rates and salary base on which the minister must base his Social Security payments. The tax rate reflects the tax credit allowed for each year.

Year	Tax Rate	Salary Base
1984	11.3%	$37,800
1985	11.8	39,300*
1986	12.3	41,700*
1987	12.3	44,100*
1988	13.02	48,800*
1989	13.02	49,800*
1990	5.3	not available

*Proposed

The unique self-employed position of the minister often creates financial hardship. His church cannot withhold Social Security taxes for him. He must calculate the tax and pay it when he pays his income taxes.

Numerous churches assist their pastors by giving them special annual allowances equal to the Social Security tax. Such an allowance is considered income, and the minister must pay income tax on it as well.

Check Your Social Security Records

As a matter of record for your family financial plan, request a Statement of Earnings from the Social Security Administration. You can do this by obtaining a Statement of Earnings postcard from your local Social Security office and mailing it to the Baltimore, Maryland, Data Center where your account is kept. When you receive your statement, verify that your earnings are correct. Any errors in your account dating three or more years back cannot be corrected.

Changing Insurance Needs

Your insurance needs will change. David and Mary are concerned about medical insurance; Robert and Lois are concerned about income replacement. The older a minister gets, the more sensitive he becomes about good medical insurance before and after retirement.

A general insurance agent makes his main commission from an ordinary or whole life policy, so he will suggest this instead of a more feasible term life policy. Know your needs. Understand the various policies. Do not make a decision until you consider the long-range implications. Medical insurance—yes! Term life insurance—yes! Disability insurance—yes! Use your salary wisely to purchase the coverage you need and avoid paying an unnecessary commission to a persuasive salesperson.

A few other comments are in order. Keep your beneficiary information current. Use well-known insurance companies. Reevaluate your coverage constantly. Use your loan values in the policies which offer them. Be very careful about canceling your medical insurance; in fact, do not cancel it until you have a satisfactory replacement.

In addition, remember that in denominations where congregational autonomy rules, it is very difficult to offer true group medical insurance. This forces some administrators to use individual underwriting, which is no problem at all to those who are healthy. But 15 percent to 20 percent of the brethren have health problems themselves or have someone in their family who does. Try to explain to a father, for example, who has an asthmatic child why the insurance carrier wants a waiver in the family policy. I can list a thousand actual cases where emotions run like a river at flood level when coverage has been denied or limited because of undeniable health problems.

In the Southern Baptist Convention, if all the churches participated in the denomination's medical insurance plan, we could eliminate instantly all underwriting, stabilize premium costs, and probably increase the coverage. But the theological truth is plain and practical—one cannot force autonomous congregations to enroll in any insurance plan. I repeat—never cancel or change medical insurance until you have a satisfactory replacement.

When you change fields of service, make certain you know your new church's insurance approach. Portability of coverage is unbelievably important.

Keep in mind that the main purpose of life insurance is to create "instant money" for your family when you die. Generally, your insurance settlement will be exempt from federal income taxes. These settlements are paid quickly in contrast to estate settlements.

Make certain your insurance coverage is right for you, then begin thinking about further investments.

6

Investing on a Small Salary

By now, the personal budget part of your financial plan depicts your current income and expenses. If these two are equal each month, you may not want to think about saving and investment strategy, but this is the very time you should be interested in this area.

Know Your Net Worth

Every successful financial plan focuses not only on the personal budget but also on net worth. Both are essential. While the personal budget reflects monthly income and expenses, net worth is the difference between what you own and what you owe. It is important that you prepare a financial statement that shows your net worth. Savings and investments should be an integral part of your net worth. It is possible that you may already be saving and investing without knowing it!

One pastor told me of a ritual he carried on for years without realizing he was saving money. Every time he received a dime, he put that ten-cent piece in a glass jar. Periodically, he took his collection of small coins to the bank, exchanging them for bills which he quickly spent. He thought nothing about what he was doing until a banker invited him to put those dimes in a savings plan. He did, and he continues to do so today. "Those dimes quickly add up," he said.

Other ways of saving are seldom considered as such. For example, your Social Security taxes are providing protection that you will use someday. The retirement program you have through your denomination and the cash value of your life insurance constitute savings. These are part of your long-range savings goals.

A sound financial plan calls for wise investing, regardless of how little it may be. In fact, the less money you have to invest, the more skill and common sense are required to manage the money. Financial ignorance comes at a high cost. The successful planner, however, keeps up with the ever-changing concepts of money management, taxation, and estate planning as he seeks ways to make his future financially sound. By wise planning now, you will avoid being one of those who will barely make ends meet in retirement.

Understanding Interest

One reason people fail in investing and savings matters is that they have not learned the basic language of the field. They dream of success but do nothing to make their dreams come true. For example, compound interest is one of the simplest principles of saving, but many people do not understand how effective it can be or how it works. You can earn interest on any amount. As you study your budget, look for places to save. Anytime you trim $5 here and $10 there, you are making progress. This may not seem like much until you put those $5s and $10s to work earning interest. The kind of interest paid on your money makes a difference, often a big one. Two basic kinds of interest are simple interest and compounded interest. Simple interest means no compounding. Suppose you deposit $100 in a savings account that pays 5.25 percent simple annual interest. At the end of one year, you will have $105.25 in your account.

Compound interest is computed continuously on a daily, monthly, quarterly, semiannual, or annual basis. When interest is compounded, you earn more on your money, depending on how often compounding occurs. Compound interest is the payment of interest on interest, as well as on the principal you own in the account. Assume you have $100 in a passbook savings account that earns a minimum of 5.25 percent interest at the savings and loan. Here is how it will grow when interest is compounded at various intervals:

How $100 Grows

When Compounded	1 Year
Daily	$105.67
Quarterly	105.467
Semiannually	105.319
Annually	105.25

The longer you leave your money in an account that earns interest, the more you will have. A simple formula that can show you how many years it takes for your money to double at any given interest rate compounded on an annual basis is often referred to as the "Rule of 72." Divide 72 by the rate of interest. The answer is the approximate number of years it will take for your money to double when the interest compounds annually. A simple formula does not exist to compute how soon your money will double when interest is compounded more frequently.

The following examples show how quickly your money can double. The calculations are approximate ones, but they are adequate for quick figuring.

Interest Paid	5%	6%	8%	10%	12%	14%
Years to Double	14.4	12	9	7.2	6	5.1

Once you master the simple principle of compound interest, you will realize that money that does not earn interest loses earnings and purchasing power. One minister's widow believed her small-town banker when he told her the main objective for her savings account was security, not return. "She knew him, and he knew her. That was the main thing." But that notion alone is naive. Although security certainly is important, making more than the banker's 5.25 percent is more important. She eventually moved her funds to another bank where certificates of deposit earned her more than 10 percent, a much better rate of return and still with the necessary security.

The following chart reflects how much interest you can earn on every $100 a year ($8.33 a month) that you save.

$8.33 Monthly Contributed for Years Indicated Accumulates to Amounts Shown

Monthly Compounding Rate	1	5	10	15	Years 20	25	30	35	40
5%	102.71	568.85	1,298.89	2,235.79	3,438.18	4,981.27	6,961.60	9,503.08	12,764.70
5.5%	102.99	576.41	1,334.79	2,332.59	3,645.41	5,372.68	7,645.27	10,635.31	14,569.32
6%	103.27	584.09	1,371.94	2,434.63	3,868.04	5,801.50	8,409.45	11,927.17	16,672.06
7%	103.83	599.85	1,450.21	2,655.70	4,364.63	6,787.26	10,221.64	15,090.30	21,992.24
8%	104.40	616.14	1,534.10	2,901.72	4,939.25	7,974.86	12,497.45	19,235.43	29,273.96
9%	104.97	633.00	1,624.06	3,175.76	5,605.22	9,408.99	15,364.47	24,688.85	39,287.86
10%	105.54	650.43	1,720.58	3,481.31	6,378.26	11,144.63	18,986.77	31,889.54	53,118.57
11%	106.12	668.46	1,824.17	3,822.30	7,276.90	13,249.64	23,576.01	41,429.47	72,296.66
12%	106.70	687.11	1,935.38	4,203.12	8,322.90	15,807.29	29,404.18	54,105.58	98,980.52
13%	107.28	706.41	2,054.84	4,628.81	9,542.12	18,920.92	36,823.65	70,997.34	136,229.87
14%	107.87	726.38	2,183.23	5,105.09	10,965.23	22,718.39	46,290.70	93,567.64	188,386.92
15%	108.47	747.05	2,321.22	5,638.27	12,627.90	27,356.34	58,391.80	123,789.16	261,593.26
16%	109.06	768.44	2,469.60	6,235.65	14,572.92	33,030.01	73,890.34	164,347.05	364,600.34
17%	109.66	790.58	2,629.25	6,905.51	16,850.99	39,981.57	93,777.22	218,891.81	509,875.53
18%	110.26	813.49	2,801.03	7,657.01	19,521.24	48,508.19	119,329.65	292,362.06	715,118.16
19%	110.87	837.21	2,985.94	8,500.73	22,654.61	58,981.00	152,213.86	391,498.99	1,005,632.00
20%	111.48	861.77	3,185.10	9,448.72	26,335.28	71,861.05	194,597.40	525,491.61	1,417,574.20

Flexible Banking Accounts

Another way for your money to grow is to use Flex, Negotiable Order of Withdrawal Accounts, or Super NOW Accounts. Banks and savings and loans offer these accounts which are similar to checking accounts except they earn interest. The main drawback is that most of these accounts require a large minimum balance. Some Super NOW, NOW, and Flex accounts will pay 5.25 percent on a balance up to $2,500 and may increase to 6.50 percent on $5,000 and up to 7.50 percent on $10,000.

One bank described its Flex account as follows:

"We pay 8.75 percent on your account if it amounts to $1,000 or more.

"We charge $5 if your account drops below $1,000 and $7 if it is less than $500. You are limited to 25 checks each month that your account is below $1,000.

"We also have a Money Market that pays 10 percent on $1,000 and lets you write three checks per month. If the account drops below $1,000, we charge $7 and reduce the interest to 9.75 percent."

One of your first goals should be to have at least 10 percent of your income deposited in a savings account. As you save, look for investments that pay a higher rate of return than a passbook account or other types of savings accounts. Make sure some of your funds remain liquid. Liquidity means you can convert the assets of the funds into cash on short notice.

Beyond savings accounts and money market funds, investing becomes more involved. Your decisions now depend on return and risk. When you lend your money, you certainly expect some return. Risk usually determines the potential return. Your money is safe in a savings account, so the rate of return is relatively low.

On the other hand, if you invest in a speculative venture, you assume a higher risk. You have no guarantee of growth nor do you have the assurance that you will not lose all of your money. Somewhere between these extremes you will find sound investing. Planning becomes very important because every dollar you spend or invest represents a financial decision you must make. You must look at the alternatives and the consequences of each possibility before you make a decision. Financial planning entails thinking ahead to the end result. Again, you must define your financial objectives before you can select the best means of achieving them. Then live with the decisions you make.

Financial Risk Is Real!

Someone once asked Baron Rothschild, one of Europe's most famous financial wizards, for investment advice. "Tell me, do you like to eat well and sleep well?" he asked. "If you like to sleep well, then don't invest in risk ventures." If you tend to worry about losses, regardless of how small, or if you do not have time to study the markets, do not consider risk ventures, such as stocks. On the other hand, if you are willing to take some risks in anticipation of greater financial rewards and if you can afford to lose, invest in common stocks or mutual funds that hold stocks. If you want no risk at all, put your money into U. S. Treasury bills and bank savings certificates.

Where Is Financial Risk?

Financial risk can be almost anywhere. A business may be financially sound today but in bankruptcy later. Good management and adequate products keep a firm in good stead, but if management, research, and products fail, the business can fail. If you own stock in a company that fails, you may lose all you have invested in what is called "equity" capital. This means that you own a piece of the enterprise, and your income increases with the success of the business. When the company folds, you are the last to receive any payment for your investment.

Purchasing power risk is a second hazard that can affect your investments. This type of risk pays you back in dollars that have been reduced by inflation. Usually such risks are found in fixed rates of return on investments such as bonds. During any period of rapid inflation, purchasing power risk must be considered.

Interest rate risk, a third type, occurs when interest rates fluctuate. Suppose you purchase bonds when interest rates are low. To sell the bonds when interest rates are high, you will have to offer them at discounts to attract purchasers, thus losing even more.

The fourth kind of risk is market risk. With this type, the market value of equities may change radically because of the investment attitude of the investors.

Investment Diversification

It is unwise to put all of your savings into one type of investment. The sound approach is to diversify for safety and protection.

First, put at least one month's income into a liquid account such as savings or a money market instrument so that the funds will be available when you need them.

Then, if you are willing to enter the investment arena by taking some risks in anticipation of greater rewards, consider investing in mutual funds, common stocks, and real estate. No one, regardless of his knowledge, can tell you the best place to invest. So, begin investing gradually. Study all you can about the investment areas in which you are interested.

Your age plays an important role in your investment strategy. A young minister will have more time to make significant gains in common stocks, mutual funds, or real estate. A minister nearing retirement will have more security with money market funds and U.S. Treasury bills which can be purchased in 13, 26, and 52-week maturities.

Your choice of investments will depend on a long-range investment plan which answers these questions:

1. What is my ultimate investment goal? How much do I need in assets and why?
2. How long will it take to reach my goals?

3. How much can I afford to invest each year?
4. Do I want to consider tax shelters?

Saving for College

David, the young seminary graduate, and his wife want to save money for college tuition for their one-year-old child. Except for buying a home, college expenses are the single largest expenditure many families have. Annual costs for a four-year education beginning in the year 2001, when the baby will start college, are estimated between $9,500 a year in a public university to $16,750 in a private institution. Approximately $67,000 will be needed to provide education for one child in a private school. David and Mary realize they must begin to save while the child is young in order to have any chance of paying tuition expenses. When college enrollment time arrives, they will also look at scholarships, government loans and grants, student employment, and school aid.

Assume David and Mary can save $1,200 a year. The following chart reflects how much they will save at various interest rates compounded annually.

$1,200 a Year with Interest Rates Compounded Annually

Interest	10 Years	15 Years	20 Years	25 Years
5%	$15,848	$27,188	$ 41,662	$ 60,135
6	16,766	29,607	46,791	69,787
7	17,740	32,265	52,638	81,211
8	18,774	35,188	59,307	94,744
9	19,872	38,403	66,918	110,788
10	21,037	41,940	75,602	129,818
11	22,273	45,828	85,518	152,398
12	23,586	50,103	96,838	179,200
13	24,976	54,806	112,164	211,020
14	26,454	59,976	124,521	248,799
15	28,018	65,660	141,372	293,654
16	29,679	71,910	160,609	346,905

If the young couple could put $100 a month in a savings plan at one of the higher rates of return shown above, their problem would be solved. But what if they could not set aside $100 a month now?

Assume David and Mary would like to save $100,000 for the college education fund and for paying off the home mortgage. Here are the factors they must consider.

Approximate Annual Deposit Needed to Equal $100,000:

Interest	10 Years	15 Years	20 Years	25 Years
5%	$7,572	$4,414	$2,880	$1,966
6	7,157	4,053	2,565	1,720
7	6,764	3,719	2,280	1,478
8	6,392	3,410	2,024	1,267
9	6,039	3,125	1,793	1,083
10	5,704	2,861	1,587	924
11	5,388	2,618	1,403	787
12	5,088	2,395	1,239	670
13	4,805	2,190	1,070	569
14	4,536	2,001	964	482
15	4,283	1,828	849	409
16	4,043	1,669	747	345
17	3,817	1,523	657	293
18	3,603	1,390	578	247

Two other methods of obtaining college expenses are through the Uniform Gifts to Minors Act (UGMA) and a Clifford Reversionary Trust.

The Uniform Gifts to Minors Act allows you to give up to $10,000 per yer in money or securities to each child without paying federal gift tax on that amount. Gift tax is assessed when property is transferred. Your spouse may also give up to $10,000 a year per child. Grandparents like the UGMA because they, too, can make this type of gift.

Under this arrangement, you can put the gift in a bank or other institution and appoint a custodian to see that the account's assets and earnings are used for the child and that the control of the account is given to the child when he or she reaches the age specified by your state. Income from the UGMA can be used for nonsupport expenses, such as education. One drawback is that you can do very little if the child does not use the money for college when he or she gets control of the account. To overcome this, name yourself as custodian. As custodian, you can distribute the income to your child. If you want to make sure the funds go for college education, set up a trust, such as the Clifford Reversionary Trust.

The Clifford Reversionary Trust is an irrevocable trust that must last for a minimum of ten years and one day or for the lifetime of the beneficiary, whichever is shorter. The trust can state that income paid to your child be used or accumulated for college educational expenses. The income is taxable, but it is based on your child's lower tax bracket. At the end of the trust period, the capital can revert to the original owner.

Determine Your Risk

Thus you can invest in three basic ways. You can make random choices, listen to sage advice from "insiders," or you can develop a strategy that leads you to investments to meet your needs.

Before you begin, decide how much you are willing to risk on each investment. If you can save only $1,200 a year, will you risk all of it on a single investment or divide it among several? If you decide to diversify, you reduce risk, but you also reduce the amounts you can invest in each category. This, in turn, reduces the possibilities of loss. For example, suppose you have accumulated $5,000 in savings. You decide to set a limit of $1,000 for any one investment. The choices that are open to you include CDs, bonds, money market funds, mutual funds, and common stocks selling under $10 a share. (Stocks usually are traded in lots of 100 shares.)

As your investment savings grow, you can increase the limits on each investment and perhaps add new ones, such as real estate properties, rental houses, and stocks valued at more than ten dollars a share.

Once you know how much money you have to invest and the amount you will allocate to each investment, set your investment priorities. Do you want cash income or growth, or a combination of both?

Finally determine the level of risk you are willing to take and the rate of return you expect.

Types of Investments

Many different investments are available, and new ones are constantly being developed. The investments presented here are the more popular ones found in individual portfolios today. Details are brief and limited because of space.

Common Stocks

Shares of common stock represent ownership in a business corporation. By investing in common stocks, you are entitled to share in the profits of the company by receiving dividends, to elect officers, to sell your shares, to experience limited liability, to examine the company books, and to share in the assets if a company is dissolved.

The market price of the stock is what investors are willing to pay for it. Two guidelines for evaluating the worth of a stock are the projected earnings and the projected dividends.

As an investor in common stock, remember several things. First, there is no legal requirement for a corporation to pay cash dividends. The board of directors can vote to reinvest the cash in the business. Second, stocks are evaluated on the stability of their earnings, dividends, and growth potential. Finally, the price of the stock is closely related to the profitability of the company, but it can be radically influenced by the investors. Common stocks usually offer good possibilities for growth, though investment in them is riskier than it is in other investments, such as bonds or preferred stocks.

Preferred Stocks

Shares in preferred stock have a fixed and usually limited return, but the return is distributed before the dividends on common stocks are paid. Unlike common stocks, preferred stocks carry no voting privileges, except when the company gets into financial trouble. Preferred stocks are better investments than common stocks for protecting your principal. But they do not offer as good a growth opportunity as common stocks do. Preferred stocks usually make better investments for corporations and big funds than they do for the individual investor.

Bonds

In the order of payment, bonds rank ahead of stocks. The issuer of bonds promises to pay fixed amounts of interest at specified times and to repay the principal. A corporation has a legal obligation to make these payments. Bonds are issued by various enterprises, including the government. A general rule is that safer investments give lower yields. Government bonds are the safest and usually pay the least. Municipals and high-grade corporates are not as safe, but the yield is greater. Bonds are usually secured by certain corporate assets, while debentures are unsecured and must depend on the reputation of the firm issuing them.

Bond prices fluctuate with market interest rates, and they are bought and sold like stocks. Like preferred stocks, bond prices usually do not fluctuate as much as common stock prices. Some corporations give buyers the privilege of converting their bonds to common stocks in the company. These are called convertible bonds because they offer the owner a fixed rate of interest and convertible privileges. Convertible bond prices will fluctuate more than the prices you pay for nonconvertible bonds. When interest rates rise, bond prices fall and vice versa. One major disadvantage of bonds for the small investor is the way bonds are traded. Usually corporate bonds are issued in $1,000 face value units. In order to receive reduced commission rates, bonds must be purchased in units of five.

U. S. Government Securities

The safest bond investment is in a U. S. government bond, including the U. S. savings bond, Treasury bond, Treasury bill, and

Treasury note. The Treasury bill, the most actively traded government security, is issued in maturities of three, six, nine, and twelve months with a minimum $10,000 investment. The T-bill is purchased on a discount basis, meaning that when you buy one, the price you pay is less than the face value. When the T-bill matures, the Treasury redeems the bond at its face value.

Other bonds do not require as much investment. The Treasury note is one that starts at $1,000 and matures in from one to ten years. The T-note is not discounted, but it pays a fixed rate of interest semiannually. Treasury bonds can also be purchased for $1,000, but they have maturity dates ranging between ten and twenty-five years. The interest that T-bonds pay varies, depending on their maturity dates and the prevailing rates when you buy them.

Money Market Funds

Money market funds offer attractive income possibilities, liquidity, and safety in varying degrees. More than three hundred money market funds are available, and they are excellent for the individual investor with a small amount of capital to invest. You can buy units for an average of $1,000, but some cost as little as $25. A major consideration in investing in money market funds is the ability to shift quickly from one fund to another within a family of funds. Many brokerage houses have a stable of investments for the individual investor with a small amount of capital to invest. For example, major houses are advertising variable packages of investments including common stocks, bonds, money market, selections of mutual funds, and government guaranteed bonds.

A *mutual fund* is a good place for a beginning investor to start. When you purchase shares, you become an indirect owner of all the securities held in the fund. This gives you a diversification which reduces your risk. Pick a fund whose investment objectives match yours. For example, if you want to take a chance on a reasonably high risk investment in hopes of earning more, invest in an aggressive growth mutual. If you do not like to take risks, desiring virtually no loss and no gain in the value of the shares, invest in a money market fund. Between these two positions are some five hundred mutual funds that strive for varying degrees of growth and income.

These are the principal kinds of securities and investments that are popular with the individual investor. Each has its advantages and disadvantages. Before you invest in stocks, study the company thoroughly by looking for strong, experienced management, strong financial position, a broad enough product mix, and a growth market for the products. Investors who have been successful in the market have done so by investing in quality securities.

Many different networks of investment possibilities exist, making it imperative that you seek the help of professionals. Large securities dealers and stockbrokers, and investment departments in banks and investment companies can provide excellent advice.

How to Begin Investing

If you are an investment beginner, you may feel overwhelmed by all of the information presented to you. So begin with your pension agency. Why? Because through this agency, your denomination is providing programs designed for ministers and their families, and it can give counsel on other financial matters. The representatives will understand your problems better than any commercial enterprise agents. Your denomination will advise you to make sure you are fully covered in the pension program and in the life, medical, and disability insurance plans. Next, purchase your own housing and do not depend on a home furnished by your church. After you have made these investments, you can move into other areas.

If you have no experience, the best place for a beginning investor is in a money market fund that has various options. This is very important when interest rates rise or fall even a percentage point or two. Defensive investments tend to roll with the interest rates and are built into the funds. They require far less complicated investment strategies than other kinds of vehicles, such as stocks.

Before you invest, know what you want. Develop your investment strategy by setting objectives that include:

1. The safety of your principal (the money you invest);
2. The income you want your investments to yield;
3. The long-term growth you want your assets to make;
4. The short-term profits you will make; and
5. The tax savings aspects open to you.

Investors must work and study continuously to be successful.
And that success comes from execution of a well-planned investment objective and from attention to possibilities and probabilities
gleaned from reading magazines, newspapers, and investment
newsletters.

Individual Retirement Account

One of the opportunities that can directly affect your plan for
saving is an individual retirement account (IRA). The law permits
any minister who is currently covered by a pension plan to establish an IRA also. You are allowed to deduct as much as $2,000 from
the taxable income you earn and put it into a special retirement
account. All earnings are also excluded from current taxes. Taxes
are deferred until you begin to withdraw funds from the account,
usually after your retirement. At that point you probably will be in
a lower tax bracket.

Your spouse can establish her own IRA provided she is em-
ployed and earns at least $2,000. If she does not earn a salary, you
may deposit a total of $2,250. This may be divided into two ac-
counts, and a minimum of $250 should be deposited into your
spouse's account. This amount can increase quickly. For example,
$2,250 a year invested at just 10 percent will grow to more than
$35,850 in ten years and almost $129,000 in twenty years.

There can be only one owner of an IRA. Wherever there is a
"spousal" IRA, the total is divided into two subaccounts. A family
with a spousal IRA should consider placing more money in the
wife's account than in the husband's account because women usu-

ally live longer than men and more wives are younger than their spouses.

The IRA is definitely a retirement savings plan. The money put into an IRA plus all it earns from interest or dividends is sheltered from income tax until it is withdrawn. You may leave your money in an IRA until age 70.5 when income tax becomes payable. While an IRA account is extremely attractive, remember that your money is locked in until age 59.5. If any of the money is withdrawn before that time, not only will you have to pay income tax on it, but you will also have to pay a 10 percent penalty on the amount withdrawn. Consult your pension agency about the most appropriate way to open or transfer an IRA.

One other word needs to be said about the individual retirement account. Available to the minister through the denominational pension board is the advantage of the tax-sheltering arrangements. This gives a minister the opportunity to contribute to a tax-sheltered annuity without the restrictions of the individual retirement account. Frankly, it is far more flexible. You can tax shelter up to 25 percent of your reportable income in this manner. If you are interested in this unique program, consult your denominational pension board about this excellent opportunity before you set up an individual retirement account.

Child Care Credits

Couples who work may be eligible to claim a credit for the costs of child care if the care is needed to enable both parents to work. Children must be under age fifteen for the credit to qualify. For tax purposes, a credit is worth more than a deduction. A dollar of tax credit directly reduces your taxes by a dollar. The value of deductions depends on your tax bracket. The value of a deduction is always less than the amount of the deduction. For example, if you had $100 in deductions, you would deduct $100 from your income before the tax is calculated. Assuming you are in the 30 percent tax bracket, your deduction of $100 will save you $30 in taxes. By contrast, a $100 credit will reduce your taxes by $100. The following chart shows the child credit allowances on taxable income.

If Your Taxable Income Is	You May Take This Amount of Credit	But the Credit May Not Exceed Number of Dependents	
		One	*Two or More*
Up to $10,000	30%	$720	$1,440
$10,001 to 12,000	29	696	1,392
12,001 to 14,000	28	672	1,344
14,001 to 16,000	27	648	1,296
16,001 to 18,100	26	624	1,248
18,001 to 20,000	25	600	1,200
20,001 to 22,000	24	576	1,152
22,001 to 24,000	23	552	1,104
24,001 to 26,000	22	528	1,056
26,001 to 28,000	21	504	1,008
28,001 and up	20	480	960

Conclusion

Keep in mind two terms: *investing* and *small salary*. Many ministers understand the latter from personal experience. Not enough ministers are yet involved in the challenge of saving through safe investment concepts. Because a minister's money is often limited, investing on his small salary mandates serious consideration of both the risks and the opportunities.

If taxes still boggle you, remember that this book is not intended to explain the tax laws in detail. Many of the provisions allowed today may be changed, modified, or eliminated by Congress during its next session.

Knowing generally what is available for investments will aid in your financial planning. From here you can decide if your personal situation requires expertise from an attorney, an accountant, or some other specialist such as a realtor. Investment in housing will be the next consideration.

7

How to Meet Your Housing Needs

By the time a minister begins serving his first church, he has made important personal decisions that affect his career, marriage, and family. Beyond these three is a decision affecting housing. The decision becomes even more important when the church provides the minister's home. There are advantages and disadvantages in occupying a parsonage or manse as David S., the new seminary graduate, and his family learned when they moved into theirs.

Advantages and Disadvantages of the Parsonage

The advantages of occupying the parsonage must begin with the cost savings. *It is nice not to have those regular mortgage or rent payments, taxes, and other costs for keeping a home in good shape,* David thought. *When the plumbing leaks or the roof needs repair, all I have to do is notify the parsonage committee of the church. When another church calls me, it will be easier to pack and leave the parsonage than it will be to move from our own home.*

Occupying a parsonage also has its disadvantages. The pastor and his family often feel they are living in a fish bowl when members drop by uninvited, expecting them to be immediately available. Also, there are times when a couple wants to change the decor but have to consult the parsonage committee first. Another major disadvantage is that a minister does not build any equity when he occupies a parsonage.

If the church you serve wants to provide a parsonage, there is little you can do to change the situation immediately. You must accept it even when you have been thinking about a home as a retirement goal. To offset this, you can put money in a savings program for that future home. An easy way to figure how much to save is to find a home where you live that you would like to own. Once you know what the monthly payments are, you can work them into your budget as savings designated for your home. Assume that you have found the house you and your family like. The payments are $500 a month. If you save $500 each month in your "home" account, earning just 10 percent interest, after the first year you will have almost $6,350; in five years, your account will total more than $39,200. Not only will you be developing a savings habit by doing this, but you will also be assured that if you get into a financial bind, you can miss a few payments without hurting your overall objective.

Housing Allowance

The Internal Revenue Code (Section 107) permits a minister to exclude from federal income taxation the rental value of a parsonage or a housing allowance paid to the extent that it is used to rent or provide a home. This is a significant tax benefit.

Ministers do not report on their federal income tax returns that part of their compensation which is designated in advance by the church or religious organizations as a housing allowance. Nor do they report the rental value of the home owned by their church which they may occupy without cost.

Who Qualifies?

Duly ordained, commissioned, or licensed ministers who are authorized to perform substantially all the religious duties of their church or denomination qualify for this tax benefit.

Religious duties include: (1) the performance of "sacerdotal functions" (for example, baptism and the Lord's Supper); (2) the conduct of religious worship; (3) the administration and maintenance of religious organizations and their integral agencies; and (4) the performance of teaching and administrative duties at theological seminaries.

The religious organizations, integral agencies, and theological seminaries must be under the authority of a religious body constituting a church or church denomination.

The Internal Revenue Service (IRS) treats commissioned or licensed ministers in the same manner as ordained ministers only when they perform "substantially" all the religious duties within the scope of the tenets and practices of their churches or denominations.

Maximum Benefits

The maximum tax benefits that can be realized are summarized as follows:

The Minister Who Owns a Home. Actual expenses incurred by a minister in providing and maintaining a home, but not to exceed either (1) church designated allowance or (2) fair rental value of home (including furnishings) plus cost of utilities.

The Minister Who Rents a Home. Actual expenses incurred by a minister in providing and maintaining a home, but in no event more than the church designated allowance.

The Minister Who Lives in the Parsonage Provided by the Church. Fair rental value of a parsonage is excludable without need of advance church designation; in addition, the actual expenses incurred by a minister in maintaining the parsonage are excludable also if the church designates a housing allowance to cover them.

Fair rental value is generally measured as the cost of renting a comparably furnished home in the minister's neighborhood. There is no universal formula for establishing fair rental value; however, in individual cases, it can be determined by consulting with local realtors.

Actual expenses may include: down payment, mortgage principal and interest payments, rental payments, real estate taxes, repairs, maintenance, yard improvements, furnishings, appliances, utilities, and homeowner's insurance. Expenses for food and maid service cannot be considered as part of the tax-free housing allowance.

Conditions. The tax-free housing allowance applies only to a "home" which must be a dwelling place, including a garage. The minister cannot exclude from gross income any amounts used in connection with a farm or other business property.

Official Designation. The housing allowance must be authorized by official action of the church or religious organization. The IRS requires designation in advance of actual payment, not in advance of the tax or calendar year. Therefore, a designation may be made at anytime; however, it will be effective only for the remainder of the year.

The official designation must be in writing and may be contained in minutes of the church business meeting, a board resolution, or in any other appropriate document.

The designation is legally sufficient if it identifies a payment of housing allowance as distinguished from salary or other remuneration. It may be stated as percentage of gross income or as a specific dollar amount.

Mechanics of Payment/Reporting. Paying a minister's housing allowance and salary in two separate checks is not necessary if proper official designation has been made.

The housing allowance (to the extent actually used to provide a home) is not reported as income and is not identified on Form 1040, Schedule C or Form W-2, nor is it reported on Form 1099 for self-employed ministers.

A copy of the official designation does not need to be attached to the tax return itself. Show the housing allowance on the Substitute for Form 2106 and retain the official designation in the employer's files.

The housing allowance or rental value of a parsonage must be included in the minister's gross income for purposes of Social Security Self-Employment Tax.

Retired Ministers. Retired ministers (but not their surviving spouses) may also qualify for a tax-free housing allowance under Internal Revenue Code Section 107 if the allowance is designated in advance and applies to retirement income received from a former denominational employer or church pension board for past services. The dollar amount eligible for exclusion is the lesser of (1) the designated amount, (2) the fair rental value of the home (including furnishings) plus the cost of utilities, or (3) the actual expenses of providing the home.

Revenue Ruling 83-3. On January 3, 1983, the IRS issued Revenue Ruling 83-3 which eliminated a double tax benefit enjoyed by minister homeowners for more than twenty years. Ministers may no longer deduct home mortgage interest and real estate taxes in addition to using their housing allowances to pay for such expenses. Now, only ministers who spend more than their designated housing allowance to provide a home will be able to deduct a proportionate share of interest and taxes for which the housing allowance was insufficient. For most ministers, the ruling will be effective January 1, 1986; for ministers who purchased a home after January 3, 1983, the effective date of the ruling was July 1, 1983.

Revenue Ruling 83-3 threatens many ministers with higher income taxes, and it may cause financial hardship.

Buy or Rent

If you are called by a church that provides a housing allowance instead of a parsonage, you must decide whether to purchase or rent a home. Advantages and disadvantages are inherent in each decision. The advantages in renting are similar to those for occupying a parsonage. The big disadvantage in renting is that you make monthly rental payments which may be higher than mortgage costs, but you accumulate no equity. However, a minister who rents can quickly and easily relocate his family in response to a call from another church, whereas as home cannot always be sold quickly. If this happens, the minister may be faced with making payments on two homes, being separated from his family until the former home is sold, or renting his former home and dealing with renters who do not pay their rent or who damage the premises.

The summary sheet reflects the economic differences between buying and renting a home.

Buy/Rent Monthly Comparison

	Buy	Rent
Rent		$ _____
Mortgage	$ _____	
Taxes	$ _____	
Utilities	$ _____	$ _____
Insurance	$ _____	$ _____
Maintenance	$ _____	
Monthly Expense	$ _____	$ _____
Less Adjustments		
Income Tax Savings	$ _____	
Appreciation	$ _____	
Equity Increase	$ _____	
NET COST	$ _____	$ _____

Home ownership can provide numerous benefits. For example, you can deduct your mortgage interest and tax payments as well as certain energy-related installations and repair costs. This will generally allow you to itemize other deductions, for example, charitable contributions and medical expenses. The deductions for the costs of home ownership allow you to reduce your taxable income significantly. Another major benefit is that you can immediately own your own property by putting a small sum of money down. Your equity will eventually become larger with each payment you make. (Equity is the total value of the property less the amount you owe.)

How Much Can You Afford for Housing?

Once you decide to purchase a home, the first thing you must do it to determine how much money to allocate in the budget for housing. Most families spend between 25 percent and 35 percent of gross income for housing. This percentage includes money for mortgage payments, taxes, insurance, maintenance, and utilities. The total of these expenditures generally approaches the percentage of income recommended by economists. The rule states that a family should spend no more than three times its gross annual income for the purchase of a home, with the total monthly housing outlay not to exceed a third of income.

Down Payment Needed

Once you and your family decide you want to buy a home, your work is just beginning. The biggest challenge is finding money for the down payment. Industry reports that more than 25 percent of all first-time home purchasers borrow from someone they know, usually parents or other relatives (not always a good idea). Once you find a benefactor, the next step is to determine how much you should request. If you are using conventional arrangements (a mortgage loan from a lending institution as opposed to government financing provided by the Veterans Administration or Federal Housing Authority), you may need 10 percent to 20 percent of the cost of the home as a down payment. If you are considering a home that sells for $100,000, you may need $10,000 to $20,000 for the initial down payment.

If you have had military service, you may be eligible of a Veterans Administration (VA) insured loan. The VA does not actually lend you money, but it will guarantee the loan will be paid if you default. It will insure your home loan for up to $27,500, which, in effect, acts as a cash down payment. If you qualify, by all means contact the VA office nearest you for complete eligibility requirements. One of the few drawbacks for a VA loan is that you may have to pay points. A point represents an immediate repayment of

1 percent of the loan, and lenders charge points to raise their effective returns. With a VA loan, the lender can charge you a one-point fee for making the loan. The lender can also charge the seller points to make up for the difference between the lower VA loan and market rates for money at the time of closing. The government says sellers are supposed to bear these costs, but the buyer usually ends up paying the points through a higher price of the home.

Another guaranteed government loan is through the Federal Housing Administration (FHA). FHA mortgages are very attractive, oftentimes making down payments as low as 3 percent. FHA loans are assumable, and they carry no repayment penalties.

Remember that your payments will be less if you make a larger down payment. Another thing to remember is never to commit all of your funds to the down payment. You may need several thousand dollars to cover closing costs, such as title changes, attorneys' fees, and mortgage points.

Mortgage Rates

Many kinds of mortgages are on the market today. You can find Adjustable Rate Mortgages, Graduated Payment Mortgages, Payment Capped Mortgages, and Shared Appreciation Mortgages in addition to the old faithful Fixed Rate Mortgage. The newest one is the Biweekly Plan Mortgage.

Adjustable Rate Mortgages (ARMs) provide for interest rates that move up or down at various intervals ranging from six months to five years. Usually, there is no limit to the rate of increase which is linked to several indexes. Ask your lender for a ten-year chart of the index used.

Graduated Payment Mortgages (GPMs) offer monthly payments that start small and gradually increase to a fixed amount. The amount of the monthly payment will change, but the interest rate never does. GPMs have been designed for young, first-time home buyers who are trying to get started in a home and who are willing to take a chance that their incomes will increase in later years.

Payment Capped Mortgages (PCMs) provide for changes in interest rates over the life of the loan, although the monthly payments are not recomputed with every change. Payments can remain fixed and are adjusted every five years. These mortgages are also known as fixed payment variables.

Shared Appreciation Mortgages (SAMs) allow the lender to provide a better rate of interest for a partial interest in the value of the home. This is not a good way to buy a home because the lender may want his share when the buyer is unable to raise the cash to buy him out.

Fixed Rate Mortgages (FRMs) are loans in which the interest rate never changes throughout the life of the mortgage. You may have the option of refinancing unless you have signed a contract that has you locked into higher rates.

Biweekly Plan Mortgages (BWMs) provide for a long-term, fixed-rate mortgage that is payable every two weeks. Each payment is about one half the standard monthly payment on a conventional thirty-year loan. The principal is repaid more quickly, resulting in lower overall interest costs over the life of the loan because by paying twenty-six times a year, the buyer makes the equivalent of thirteen payments instead of twelve. You probably will want to consider another plan if you intend to stay in your home for only a few years.

Be careful of the "creative financing mortgage." This type of mortgage was designed to shift the risk of long-term financial commitment from the lender to the buyer. Some of the newer types of mortgages contain more risk for the buyer than before.

Avoid a due-on-sale clause in your mortgage loan contract if you can. Due on sale means the entire mortgage balance becomes payable in one lump sum if you sell the property to someone else. The person who buys your property is not allowed to assume your mortgage.

Never accept a "call option" clause. This occurs when the lender can call the loan in a certain number of years by canceling it or by renewing it with higher interest rates if the market dictates. There is no ceiling on how high the interest rate might go, even if the lender states he will guarantee to renew the loan. Always consult your real estate broker or attorney for guidance if you are interested in this type of loan.

Buying a home can be a great investment opportunity for a minister, especially if he manages it properly. We see this in the life of William P., the sixty-two-year-old minister whose home will be cleared of debt in a short time. He is also trying to decide whether to sell and move nearer his daughter after he retires. His home is valued at $90,000 with $8,000 left to pay on a 6.5 percent mortgage. He contemplated paying off the mortgage. Instead, he invested the money in a money market fund, giving him greater personal liquidity.

Advantages of Prepaying

By contrast, Rev. A. is saving thousands of dollars in interest simply by following a little-known and seldom-used procedure of adding a few extra dollars each month to his mortgage payment.

Rev. A. has a $50,000 mortgage at 14 percent. Under the normal payment plan for 30 years, he would pay a total of some $213,000. He figured that by voluntarily adding an extra $50 to the principal each month, he could cut his total cost to $132,000 and pay off his mortgage in 17 years.

Before voluntarily making payments on your principal, carefully study your situation. Ask what your lending institution requires for prepaying and if it has any penalties or fees for doing this.

Some lending agencies promote prepayment by having a special line on the mortgage payment slips to record additional payments on the principal. All you have to do is fill in the amount you are sending.

Prepaying will have tax implications concerning the interest line if you itemize deductions. Your interest deduction will be greatly reduced in the later years of the mortgage.

This procedure depends entirely on the buyer. You can stop paying extra on the principal if your economic situation requires it, or you can increase to a larger amount if you receive a tax refund or some type of financial gift.

Prepaying requires discipline since you alone must motivate yourself to act upon it. Your lending agency does not require it, but it may allow you to do so.

Picking the Right House

"A man's home is his castle," penned the sage. When you decide to buy, take your time and consider a number of factors in selecting your castle. Take into account the location, construction, floor plan, and space utilization.

Of all of these, location is the most important. You could have the finest constructed home, but if it is located in a deteriorating neighborhood, you could have a bad purchase.

Decide whether you want a new home or an older one. Some people prefer older homes because of their charm and because they can be remodeled to suit the new owner's wishes. Others prefer new homes without the problems that go with making an older home livable. Remember, it is your castle. What do you want?

Conclusion

No easy answers are available to the many questions about housing for the minister. Pros and cons are on both sides of the issue—the parsonage versus the housing allowance. Keep in mind that before retirement or after, the advantages of owning your own home accelerate. Laws governing the minister's housing allowance will continue to tilt toward federal authorities, but the need for independent housing will grow. Chapter 8 will expand on the need for ministers to own their own homes.

In your financial planning, structure your hopes and dreams for your family's housing. A church parsonage may meet some real needs in the early years of ministry. This was my experience. Then came the call to Dallas's Cliff Temple Baptist Church in the mid-sixties, just at the point when my family financial needs were moving into high gear. I followed Dr. Wallace Bassett at that church, a man who probably had the earliest minister's housing allowance in the denomination. The pulpit committee simply told me I had to make arrangements for housing. After living in four parsonages, this was a new wrinkle.

The big issue for me was getting enough money together for a down payment. Fortunately, we had a small nest egg, but I felt nervous about disturbing it. It turned out not only to be a very good investment, but it also gave the entire family a delightful pride in ownership, stability, and identity. What for us was momentarily very difficult turned out to be a genuine "blessing in disguise."

This experience, more than any other, helped me as a pastor to understand what other staff members go through in the housing crisis. Churches make provisions for pastors, but they often are unaware of the crisis the rest of the staff experiences. The bottom line, again, is awareness of the issues, planning far ahead, involving the entire family.

My own conclusion is that more churches are now sensitive and concerned about the housing problem that the pastor and the staff face. Housing costs have skyrocketed, and there is no hint that prices will moderate. Many multistaff churches have failed to attract key staff members because of the housing problem. I am glad to note that more of the laity are aware of this essential financial challenge, and they are taking concrete steps to assist the staff in this area. Although staff members are grateful for this consideration, they will be even more grateful when they come to retirement!

8

Financial Planning
for Retirement

Three elements are essential to successful retirement, with each of them related to the basic rules for successful financial planning. First, have enough money to live on without extensive worry. Second, have a reasonable degree of health. Third, have a continuing purpose for living. All are important and related. Perhaps the second and third are in some degree contingent upon the first. Each is within the bounds of preparation during the minister's years of service. Although the younger minister will think less of the amount of retirement income than the older one, problems emerge if one fails to begin early.

To assure financial adequacy during retirement, let me share with you eleven rules. These rules are directed specifically to the minister and his wife. Some of them apply to the laity; but, as you will see, the minister has some special challenges in retirement preparation.

One interesting fact which mandates attention is the highly encouraging news that ministers live longer than any other professional group. This longevity behooves them to do a better job of planning than any other group. Generally, ministers retire with small annuities because their salaries are, on an average, among the lowest of all professions. This limitation also makes careful planning essential.

First, let me list the rules. Then we shall look at them carefully.

1. Plan to live on less money in retirement.
2. Plan ahead for financial security in retirement.
3. Remember the impact of inflation on a fixed income.
4. Structure an emergency fund in your financial planning.

5. Keep an accurate record of your expenditures at least two to four years before retirement, and keep them during retirement.
6. Rethink your insurance needs.
7. Plan your housing requirements, combining dreams with common sense, but plan!
8. Increase your recreation budget.
9. Take advantage of the tax laws in retirement.
10. Rethink your will.
11. Relax now and enjoy your retirement years when they come.

A nationally known pastor who retired several years ago commented on his situation in retirement:

> I wish I had some soap box to get on to tell younger and middle-aged preachers how happy and relaxed the retirement years are. I surely would bear down hard on planning financially for those years. My wife and I did, and it is thrilling to see our financial planning produce just plain happiness.

Rule Number One
Plan to Live on Less Money in Retirement

You can do it—if you really desire. Income tax demands will be reduced in retirement. Also, Social Security payments, which are a real burden for the self-employed minister, will change to a plus. You are finally receiving, not giving.

You can get by with one car. It may be inconvenient until you get used to it if you have been a two-car family, but you can pocket real savings if you have only one car parked in the garage. Consider the cost of the vehicle, insurance, basic operation, repairs. Savings can add up in a hurry. This arrangement may be harder on your wife than on you, but at least consider it.

Many ministers in retirement have actually discovered that they can cut down significantly on new clothes and entertainment expenses. Some have found that they do not need as many books and magazines in retirement. Others have also realized that they have time to take advantage of the services of the local public library.

Please do not interpret these suggestions as a negative approach to ministerial retirement. They apply to any retired person. Corners can be cut that will not cut the quality of life. There is real adventure in discovering that you can get by on less.

Planning to live on less should be done three to five years before retirement, with both mates agreeing to the reductions. A one-sided approach can be distinctly unpleasant. But the rule holds firm—plan to get by on less. (This is not a bad rule for any stage of life.)

Rule Number Two
Plan Ahead for Financial Security in Retirement

This rule is of cardinal importance because your financial situation in retirement will affect recreation, housing, and insurance. In fact, it will affect your whole style and standard of living. It is not enough to say that you must have enough money coming in after retirement to enable you to live as you want to live; you must have a strategy that permits you to follow through.

Here we are again at the basic level of financial planning, the budget! Income for the average minister in retirement includes denominational pension, Social Security, interest and dividends, or possibly inheritance. The following chart can be used to estimate your income:

My Proposed Retirement Income

	Monthly	Annual
Projected Denominational Annuity	_____	_____
Projected Social Security	_____	_____
Estimated Interest, Dividends, etc.	_____	_____
Other	_____	_____

A rule of thumb is to have a minimum of 70 percent of your pre-retirement salary coming in at retirement. This level of income will

permit you to retire on basically the same standard of living you
had before retirement. One reason for this is that according to rule
number one, your expenses can actually decline.

One problem for the minister in retirement is recognizing the
difference between what your retirement income will be and what
you need. How do you cope with this retirement gap? If the gap is
too large, you may have to continue working. Your spouse may
have to continue working. A minister has some fine opportunities
to increase his income in retirement by continuing to pastor a
smaller church, or by preaching on an interim or supply basis, or
by turning skills and hobbies into paying propositions (child care,
pet care, house-sitting, odd jobs). Moving to an area where there
are very few ministers available for supply work affords distinct
opportunities.

On the other hand, one must inform himself concerning the
amount that he can profitably earn. Some of the best information
on Social Security is in *Your Retirement—A Complete Planning Guide*
by the editors of *Consumer Guide*. The chapter entitled "Getting
the Most from Social Security" is well worth the price of the book.

Many ministers have discovered that the "self-employed"
record-keeping section of Social Security runs behind the regular
members' section in providing information. Check the accuracy of
your records every three years. If no question is asked within
three years, the records become a permanent, unchangeable part
of your Social Security history. A good address to keep in mind is
the Social Security Administration, Department of Public Inquir-
ies, 6401 Security Boulevard, Baltimore, Maryland 21235. Practically every telephone directory has the address of the local office.
The people who serve in the local office are generally very responsive and helpful.

The other major part of the minister's retirement comes from his
denominational pension plan. Practically all denominational pension boards send their members an annual projection of what they
can expect at age sixty-five, the normal year for retirement. They

will also project the benefit at other ages, both before and after sixty-five.

Most denominational pension plans permit tax sheltering a minimum of 25 percent of your cash income, excluding the housing allowance. Practically all church pension boards operate under Section 403(b) of the Internal Revenue Service Code. This generous tax-sheltering provision for churches and non-profit institutions meets most of the needs of employees herein affected. Add to this the equivalent individual retirement account and you can add substantially to your retirement income if you plan your strategy carefully. Fortunate, indeed, are the ministers who may have extra sources of income beyond Social Security and their own pensions. Some have an inheritance which helps with income. Others have investments in stocks, bonds, and real estate. All of these need to figure in the retirement income schedule. Financial security in retirement is a matter of strategy and putting that strategy to work. Planning with limited resources is an additional essential challenge.

Rule Number Three
Remember the Impact of Inflation on a Fixed Income

The Rule of 72 in the aforementioned *Your Retirement—A Complete Planning Guide* can help you determine what your dollars will be worth when you retire.[1] Use an annual inflation rate of 8 percent—not unreasonable in our current economy. Divide 72 by 8; the answer is 9. This means that in nine years what you buy will cost twice as much. At an annual inflation rate of 6 percent, your dollar will split in half twelve years later. Inflation is figured at 4 percent to 6 percent annually over the long term, but the inflation rate recently has been more than 12 percent.

The reason I am stressing this particular rule is that most planners leave out the inflationary factor when they come to the specific dollar amount for retirement income. Projections given to future annuitants state that they will receive a specific dollar amount. The Rule of 72 simply mandates the absolute necessity of considering inflation in retirement financial planning.

Let's take a 5 percent inflation factor which is extremely conservative in today's uncertain economy. In ten years time, a 5 percent factor will eat away 50 percent of your retirement dollars. Let me illustrate this specifically. Suppose your combined Social Security and denominational pension total $10,000 a year in retirement. For a minister who received $20,000 as a salary, $10,000 sounds like an excellent pension. If inflation is at a conservative level of 5 percent after your retirement, remove $1,000 in buying power. To put it bluntly, this hurts savagely when you are on a fixed income. Although Social Security has a cost-of-living factor in it, its continuance is increasingly uncertain in today's world of governmental deficits. Most denominational pensions and annuities from life insurance policies are fixed. The only potential for increased benefits at this level comes from outstanding investment results, but experience indicates that such is relatively unlikely. Add to this the encouraging and frequently heralded breakthroughs in medical science which extend longevity, and there is an increasing trend toward conservative projections in the fixed income area. People are living longer, and this has to be considered when settlements are made on annuities.

The practical application of the Rule of 72 is to put as much money as possible aside for your retirement income before you retire. This is not easy for the minister. In our studies of the five preachers, only William, age sixty-two, was tax sheltering part of his denominational salary to catch up, hoping for a reasonable retirement income.

Again, the best time to begin financial planning is in your younger years of service. Being aware of the Rule of 72 should mandate the younger minister's doing what the older minister is unable to do—invest more in a retirement annuity plan.

One of the problems in some of the good retirement planning comes in the antagonism between the older minister and the younger minister. In some church staffs, the older minister has seen healthy projections of the younger minister's retirement income. (The increases occur because of an increased participation in the denominational pension plan and because of higher rates of interest that investment vehicles have produced in recent years.) The older minister, then, has seen salaries and retirements that exceed his current salary, and he becomes confused, perhaps even angry. I recall one man who wanted to change the whole plan because of this. "This would be too much money for those younger ministers." My response was immediate and rather forceful. "Who can tell thirty years from now what the rate of inflation will be. Even if you receive 100 percent of your salary at retirement, what will you have in fifteen or twenty years?" The older man saw the wisdom of that planning and actually changed his opinion!

Rule Number Four
Structure an Emergency Fund in your Financial Planning

Sometime in your retirement years, you will face a financial emergency. As part of your preparation for this, have $10,000 to $15,000 in cash, or its equivalent, drawing interest in an accessible account.

Five to ten years before retirement, begin setting this money aside as a part of your financial plan. Decide the purpose of the fund, keeping in mind that it should be used for a real emergency.

Put the money to work in a savings and loan deposit, a credit union, or certificates of deposit, but do not put it in investment vehicles that cannot be transferred into cash quickly and easily.

One of the key laws to watch in retirement financial planning is the high cost of small loans. An emergency fund will head this off.

Contingency planning mandates agreement between the minister and his wife about the use of this emergency fund. A basic rule is that it is "a last resort." One minister and his wife had the unpleasant experience of having their car totaled in a highway accident. They were grateful they were not injured, but they faced the emergency of needing a car. They agreed that the difference between the insurance settlement and the cost of the new car should be drawn from their emergency fund. A second step was to try to replenish the fund with monthly additions.

Rule Number Five
Keep Accurate Records of Your Expenditures
Two to Four Years Before Retirement and
Keep Them During Retirement

Planning for financial security in retirement grows out of planning for financial security before retirement. The charts shown in chapter 3 should be completed as you near retirement. Look carefully at your present income. Consider the changes to come your way five to ten years before retirement. Scrutinize how you spend your money. This sounds easy, but for those who are undisciplined in these matters, it is sometimes irritating, time consuming, and frustrating. Use the Retirement Budget Planning Worksheet to assist you in recording your expenditures.

Retirement Budget Planning

Expenditures	Before Retirement *Monthly*	Estimated After Retirement *Annual*
Housing Costs (if you own your home) Or Estimated Parsonage Allowance	$_____	$_____
Insurance	_____	_____
Automobile	_____	_____
Food	_____	_____
Clothing	_____	_____
Health Care	_____	_____
Personal Care	_____	_____
Recreation	_____	_____
Contributions	_____	_____
Misc. (gifts, etc.)	_____	_____

Income

Annuity Savings   _____   _____

Social Security   _____   _____

Income Tax   _____   _____

Other Insurance, Savings   _____   _____

After keeping these records for several years, study them for trends. Put rule number five against rule number one. Where can you live on less? Remember, every family is different. Set goals that apply to your personal needs.

Rule Number Six
Rethink Your Insurance Needs

Retirement marks a watershed in insurance planning, especially for health insurance. Needs change markedly with aging. I mentioned at the outset of this chapter that one of the most important aspects of a successful retirement is having health enough to enjoy it. But health maintenance comes as a priority long before retirement. Few habits mark modern America as much as its consuming interest in personal well-being. Older people are living longer and enjoying it because they have taken better care of themselves physically than any generation in human history. But preventive medicine is not all.

One of your major concerns as you rethink your insurance needs in retirement is to make certain that you have enough health and medical insurance. Survey after survey confirms that the fear of having a major illness with inadequate hospitalization benefits is one of a retiree's top concerns.

In the American system, the basic health insurance program is Medicare, a vital part of the Social Security system. Though Congress changes Medicare cost allowances almost annually, it still is basic to your retirement financial planning.

Medicare has two main levels of coverage—hospitalization insurance and medical insurance. Medical insurance is optional, and you pay a monthly premium for it. When you begin receiving

Social Security benefits, you are automatically eligible for Medicare benefits. One thing to keep in mind is that Medicare does not pay for everything. The percentage of covered expenses decreases every year, and the cost increases, but the basic point remains: Medicare's health coverage provides the main basis for covering medical costs after retirement.

Despite all of the bad news about the continuing financial crisis in Social Security and Medicare, there is little danger that we will lose all of these benefits. It is too vital a part of the American system. The political power of the elderly is too large for any politician to stop these programs. More than that, the needs are so great that it will always be a part of retirement planning.

As you rethink your insurance needs, invest in a Medicare supplemental insurance program. Most of the general denominational insurance plans offer a "Medicare-Senior Citizens" supplemental policy or a maintenance-of-benefit concept upon retirement. Be sure that you are enrolled in the plan before retirement because it is very difficult and quite expensive to obtain coverage after retirement.

Many other policies are available for elderly people, generally offered by mail. Be very careful about enrolling in them. Some of them are excellent; some are not. Check some helpful sources before you begin this kind of investing.

Experiences abound about elderly people who have taken out two, three, even four separate supplemental policies. Many of them are designated for specific illnesses, such as cancer. Some are direct cash payments to the person in the hospital. One minister I know almost rejoices about an illness because he makes money from it!

Though hospitalization and health insurance constitute a major concern of rethinking your insurance needs, this is not the only area for consideration. When you draw your retirement income, payments for disability insurance cease. Term insurance, which basically is income protection, is no longer needed in retirement. You need to examine a whole life insurance policy, which might have been taken out decades before retirement. Check to see if there are costly monthly premiums until death. Large insurance premiums during retirement years can be a drain on your finances.

Make your plan with personal requirements in mind. A minister in a deep-South city took retirement two years early because of a heart condition. He made complete plans to have adequate medical insurance. A close relationship with a deacon doctor brought home the sad news that his years of life were limited. Knowing this prompted him to keep intact his entire life insurance policies, the plans he had taken out years before. Many of us are unaware of the radical change in insurance products, sensing somehow that whole life policies with premiums due to death are the major approach.

This rule is complex but important: Rethink *your* insurance needs.

Rule Number Seven
Plan Your Housing Requirements, Combining
Dreams and Common Sense, but Plan

Few decisions in retirement are more important than where you live. It can open the door to many new and exciting possibilities for the minister and his wife. Often, the housing decision for the minister in his active years is one over which he has no control.

As you plan for retirement, one of the key elements of your plan is to dream about your ideal choice in housing, then put feet to your dreams. Each situation is unique, requiring individual considerations, but some general guidelines will help in your planning.

First, consider moving away from your church field. Do this for personal freedom rather than the older issue of getting out of the new pastor's way. Though no actual survey of this issue has been made, studies in the area of general retirement indicate that nearly 50 percent of retirees would have chosen to move if they had the finances.

A pastor I saw not long ago had announced his retirement three months hence. He had lived in a beautiful church parsonage in the same field for the last twenty-five years. Some of the members of the church wanted to give the house to him in gratitude for his years of sacrificial service. When the church met to consider this, it became an instant occasion for contention. The gracious pastor simply closed the issue. The only consideration the church gave him was the privilege of staying in the home until the new pastor arrived. He confided to me with deep emotion that this kind of cloud hanging over him was the most painful thing he had faced in retirement preparation. He later told me he had found a small home less than a mile from the parsonage. I strongly asked about the advisability of staying on the church field where he had served so long. "We have considered it seriously; I won't do funerals and weddings, but this route seems to be the best for us because of continued opportunities for supply and interim work." Yet refusing to help old friends in life's crises is not easy if one is nearby.

The minister who lives in church-owned housing needs to think seriously about moving out of the community when he retires. "Out of the community" does not mean an immigration to another state. It can be to a community five or ten miles away.

The minister who buys his own residence with the church-provided housing allowance faces the delightful option of staying right where he is or of selling and relocating. This kind of freedom is exhilarating. Purchasing your own home during your active ministry provides far more than the satisfaction of homeownership. In retirement, it opens the door for additional choices in housing. One major tax advantage the homeowner has is the one-time privilege after age fifty-five of selling the house and pocketing tax free up to $100,000 in capital gains tax. Many retirees have taken advantage of this tax option, invested the returns, and enjoyed additional income in retirement. Some have discovered that leasing or renting has advantages, particularly if extended absences for travel or resident interim ministries are involved.

At retirement, most people prefer to reside near family and friends. The minister, however, has the problem of having lived in a number of places. Often, the area where he resides at retirement is not where he wants to stay. Here is a place to put down a cardinal law in housing and moving in retirement: Do not follow your children! They can and do move themselves. A good rule of thumb is to locate less than a day's drive away.

Another key point to keep in mind is that part of the minister's denominational pension can be designated as housing allowance. As such, it is considered tax-free income. But take vital note: This benefit is available *only through the denomination's pension plan.* It does not accompany an individual retirement account or an insurance annuity. Social Security is not involved. When a minister reaches retirement age, practically all church pension boards request a housing designation which allows the retiring pastor to choose up to 100 percent of his pension for housing allowance purposes.

With all these considerations, let us come back to some of the basics in planning your housing requirements for retirement. I mentioned at the outset using common sense, which begins at your front door. What works for one may not work for another. For example, do not buy a two-story town house next door to your children if your wife has arthritis and cannot climb stairs, even though you enjoy the grandchildren. It appeals to some to leave the church field in retirement and move to Florida or South Texas, but do you make new friends easily? Will there be medical facilities if you need them? Common sense requires doing a great deal of study and preliminary groundwork. Climate enters into the picture. Proximity to family and friends is vitally important. Do not move to a new place until you know the tax base. Are recreational opportunities available? Is a good public library nearby? What about cultural enjoyment, shopping centers? Are there opportunities for preaching, supply or interim work? The list grows, but each issue must be addressed. Above all, answer the question,

Can you afford what your dreams dictate? No one can make these plans for you, but the rule is still firm: Plan your housing requirements with dreams and common sense.

One other word: Do this preliminary work at least five to ten years before your retirement date. You will be glad you did.

Rule Number Eight
Increase Your Recreation Budget

Retirement means freedom from routines, schedules, and meetings. Time is available for travel, hobbies, visiting family and friends. It is important to budget for this. Most ministers have had limited travel resources and scant time for this enjoyable phase of life. The more you can plan and experiment with this in the years leading up to retirement, the more likely it is you will enjoy this facet of retirement. A fine preacher I knew was always making plans to travel in retirement. His children kept telling him that he needed to travel before retirement, but an extremely busy round of responsibilities, seemingly, made it impossible. The family reminded him often that if he did not travel before retirement, he might not travel after retirement. His response was to plead the pressure of time. When he retired, he was given money to go to the Holy Land. He planned to go, but other priorities kept crowding it aside. The family finally decided that he was in retirement what he had been before. They finally accepted it because it was the way he wanted it.

Another minister and his wife planned for years before retirement to schedule one trip abroad and one extended trip in the States every year. They listed what they wanted to see, clipped material on it, kept files, and discovered the excitement of planning, as well as the joy of fulfillment. Even more important, they budgeted for these plans by expanding that part of their financial dream.

Recreation means far more than travel. It also includes the pursuit of hobbies that range from the familiar fishing, gardening, collecting, and golfing to literally hundreds of other interests—

ceramics, art, photography, and antiques, to mention a few. If you live in a metropolitan area, visit your community college and discover what it offers in noncredit classes. Not all hobbies cost a great deal of money. One minister invested in some binoculars and joined a society of bird-watchers. It has brought him, with very little financial investment, to a genuinely fulfilling hobby.

Do not wait until retirement to develop your hobbies and interests. Naturally, these will change, but the rule still applies: Plan to increase your recreation budget in retirement. Be creative; be aware of the opportunities available.

Perhaps this is a good place to suggest that many ministers have difficulty personally and theologically with too much leisuretime. Ordination is for life, and your retirement does not eliminate the daily need for Christian service. A recent survey by the American Association of Retired Persons found that, on the average, one out of three retired persons would rather be working. Another part of the survey proved that the preference for retirement (and its attendant leisure) increased as retirement income increased.

Ministers with limited retirement annuities who are deeply committed to the ministry may have real difficulties (not imagined at all) with the rule to increase the recreation budget. My advice is to try anyway!

Rule Number Nine
Take Advantage of the Tax Laws in Retirement

Numbers of older Americans are overpaying their federal taxes because they do not know some of the laws specially designed to help retired persons. A key rule in retirement is to study such laws. Cultivate an accountant who can help you. Call the local Internal Revenue Service office and ask for information and advice.

Let me list some special tax benefits for older citizens. You have been taking a personal exemption of $1,000 on your income tax form. If you are sixty-five or older, you can deduct $2,000. This applies to the minister and to his spouse if each is sixty-five.

If you or your spouse are fifty-five or older, remember the exceptional blessing available in a one-time sale of your home. Suppose you paid $50,000 for a home fifteen years before retirement. You and your wife decide you want to move closer to your children. Then comes the pleasant discovery that your house has substantially appreciated to an appraisal of $100,000. If you are past fifty-five, you make a $50,000 profit, and it is not subject to income tax. You must live in your home at least three of the five years before the sale. Check with your tax accountant for all the details on this. Other additional rules are in place for persons who sell their homes after age sixty-five. Some fortunate ministers have taken advantage of this relatively new law and have increased their incomes by investing that additional amount in a certificate of deposit, for example. Seek the advice of an accountant who knows the tax rules applicable to the ministry.

One of the biggest areas for saving after sixty-five is in the amount of income tax you pay. Social Security benefits will probably be tax free for most ministers because of small retirement annuities. However, Social Security benefits are subject to tax since 1984 if other annuities total $25,000 or more. Most ministers do not have to worry about this because of their relatively low annuities.

Keep an accurate record of your medical expenses. Most medical deductions are subject to the rule of 3 percent, which means you can deduct 3 percent of your taxable income. Keep an accurate record of all medicines, prescriptions, and treatments recommended by your doctor.

Remember that the laws are changing constantly, and frequently they change in favor of the older citizen. Politicians are well aware of the political clout of this group and are quite open and responsive in assisting because of the peculiar needs of retirees. One of the best sources of information is the American Association of Retired Persons.

Rule Number Ten
Rethink Your Will

An updated will is always a basic part of the thinking minister's financial plan, before and after retirement. Rethinking your will is important because conditions always change. Ministers' families are not immune, for example, to the problem of divorce. One minister had not updated his will for nearly twenty years. He and his wife were crushed when their only son had an ugly divorce, an event which caused much family unrest. Their daughter-in-law received custody of the grandchildren. The minister's will as written mandated a settlement favoring the first wife over the second. A family friend suggested a restudy of the will, resulting in some long overdue action which eventually saved both money and emotion. Unhappy stories result where ministers or their widows do not think about changing an obsolete will or ignore making a will at all. Good stewardship demands that you protect your assets and make certain that your possessions are left as you desire.

Despite the minister's exposure to helping his members set up wills, many die intestate. Simply stated, *intestate* means death occurs without a valid will. When this happens, the state steps in and tells how the possessions are to be distributed. Because the laws vary from state to state, it is hard to cover all the bases here. Horror stories abound about insensitive probate courts determining the best division of the property. Many people can tell about the delays of months, even years, in settling relatively small estates. May I make a strong appeal to go to a reputable attorney and make a will if you have not done so. It simply is unfair and unchristian to put your survivors through anguish, confusion, and embarrassment because you did not plan ahead. If you do not make a will, the state will make your will and then charge your estate for its expenses.

Make certain your will is current. List your specific requests. Appoint someone to be the executor of your estate and make sure the language in the will empowers the executor to determine what should be done if it is not covered in the main body of the will. Give that executor the power to pay all claims.

It is not a bad idea to divest yourself of some of those precious possessions before death. Know the joy of giving those books, heirlooms, and other valuables to people or institutions who you know will appreciate them. Do not ever create issues after your death because of your poor stewardship.

Tell someone where your will is kept. Give copies of the will to your executor and your attorney. Appoint a backup executor. Do not write in changes to your will; go back to your lawyer and consider it a wise investment to do it right so that challenges will not come. More ministers are realizing that the size of their estates is larger than they anticipated. Many wills have been changed to add a percentage of the assets to a favorite institution or church.

One of the major reasons for keeping your will updated is to protect your assets. It is good stewardship and good religion to do so.

Rule Number Eleven
Relax Now and Enjoy Your Retirement
Years when They Come

Read J. Winston Pearce's superb work, *Ten Good Things I Know About Retirement*. It is just what ministers and spouses need to cap their commitment about retirement planning. Confirming that bit of advice is a statement from one of the best books the American Management Association ever published. *"The basis for a satisfactory life in retirement lies in determining what all the options are, deciding which ones to pursue and how to pursue them, and finally acting on these decisions.* With this kind of planning, your new way of life can be very attractive."[2] By following the rules, you can plan and expect a most attractive period of life after the active years of the pastorate. But planning comes right down to the individual; *you* have to do the planning. Set goals and bring them into a workable and personal approach. Put emotion to one side and make decisions based on facts, but include a margin for error. Then provide for flexibility, and constantly review your plan.

Notes

1. Consumer Guide, *Your Retirement—A Complete Planning Guide*, (New York: A & W Publishers, Inc., 1981).

2. Robert K. Kinzel, *Retirement—Creating Promise out of Threat*, (New York: American Management Association, 1979), p. 67.

9

More About Your Wills
and the Future

The final step in a successful financial plan is to make a will and keep it updated. A will is absolutely essential if you are concerned about who will get your property and assets when you die. In fact, your financial plan should entail wills for all adults in your family, including you, your spouse, parents, and all children eighteen years or older.

The First Step

The first step to take in preparing a will is to consult an attorney. Do not try to write a will yourself. A handwritten will is legal in less than half of the fifty states, and often it is difficult to establish the validity of such wills in those states. A judge once commented that a will written without legal counsel is an open door to litigation.

Why is a will necessary? Because every estate, large or small, must be settled by law. If you want your family or certain organizations to share in what you have accumulated, state your desires in a legal instrument that will stand up in court. Anticipate every situation that can arise, and make sure you are complying with all of the laws of *your* state pertaining to wills. Your attorney will ensure your will is correct.

By contrast, if you die without a will (called intestate), everything you own will be distributed by the impersonal laws of your state. It is estimated that eight out of ten people die without wills. It is also estimated that more than one half of all wills are outdated because of the many changes that have been made in the law, and more than one third are outdated because of changes in personal possessions!

Seven Essential Steps

Before you talk with your attorney, do some personal planning, thinking, and sharing about these areas.

1. Discuss with your spouse and your children how you want your property distributed. Tell them what you hold in assets and liabilities, how you want the property to be divided, and to whom and why.

2. Put in writing how you want your property to be divided and to whom and why. Have your spouse do the same thing. Every woman should have her own will, regardless of her amount of personal property.

3. Assemble and keep all valuable papers pertaining to property deeds, mortgages, agreements, contracts, insurance policies, certificates, and so forth where they can be found quickly. The safest place, of course, is a safe deposit box.

4. Update the list of names and addresses of your beneficiaries. This list can include members of your family, friends, charities, institutions, or other particular causes.

5. Keep your personal financial records current.

6. Make sure your family will have money available if you die suddenly. This will ensure that they will not have to sell some property, maybe at a loss, to make ends meet.

7. Make the appointment with an attorney for you and your spouse.

Laws pertaining to wills vary from state to state. When you move from one state to another, have an attorney check your will and bring it into compliance with your new location. If you live in a community property state, you must have a will if you want others to share in the distribution of your property. Otherwise, all of your assets will go to your surviving spouse. Community property states include Arizona, California, Idaho, Louisiana, Nevada,

New Mexico, Texas, and Washington, and in them all property is owned equally by husband and wife. Exceptions to this include assets acquired by each before marriage, gifts or inheritance, and compensation received from an injury. It is very important that you keep good records if you live in one of these states because, when there is a doubt, the legal system of the state will consider everything in the estate as community property.

Preparation of a will is not expensive. Fees generally range from $100 to about $300 for a relatively simple will. Even if you have a large and complex estate, you can lower your fees by giving your lawyer accurate and well-organized guidelines about how you and your spouse want your property and assets distributed. The Minister's Data Checklist in the appendix will help you put on paper the information you need.

Updating Your Will

Review your will periodically to make sure you are satisfied with the distribution and to conform with changes in federal and state laws. The following three steps are important in motivating you to update your will.

When You Move to Another State

Your permanent residence when you die determines the law that applies to the distribution of your property. You may have a valid will in the state from which you moved, but it may not be recognized in your present state. The property you own, even bank accounts, may be distributed as if you had never prepared a will. *Update your will by making it applicable to the state in which you are living.*

When Your Family Circumstances Change

If your will is written properly to divide your property equally, you may not need to update it when new children and grandchildren are born. You will need to revise it if major changes are made in your marital status.

When Financial Conditions Change

As your assets and properties increase or decrease, make appropriate changes to your will. Consider using percentage allocations, not dollar amounts, to keep from having problems.

Minister's Data Checklist

It is important that all your family documents and records be protected in a safe place, such as a bank safe deposit box. Someone other than you should know where these valuable documents are located.

The checklist in the appendix is designed to help you record a detailed history of all the data pertaining to your family and personal records. Make several copies of this checklist and tell family members where they are kept.

Some of these forms may seem unnecessary. If you think so, let me suggest that you talk to a new widow. Rather blunt idea, isn't it? But some people have to pull this information together at the worst of times due to an accident or an unexpected death. One other suggestion is to use these guides for putting the answers on a tape cassette which you can update annually.

Ministers should not conclude that they are the only ones who are reluctant to plan financially. Probably they are far better at organizing than others. This is a good place to suggest that you use your teaching opportunities to encourage financial planning in your church family ministries. The needs are endless; the rewards can result in stability and fulfillment.

10

Enduring Financial Guidelines

Like it or not, we in the ministry must deal with money! We have no choice. We will do it well, or we will do it poorly. How we handle it will influence us personally and professionally, and this influence will spill over into every facet of family life.

In these chapters, I have sought to major on a few of the obvious areas of interest and application. Not only are there many more areas clamoring for attention but there are also dozens of other subdivisions in the subjects treated. Let me review with you eight basic ground rules which may help you as a minister to be a good financial manager.

Remember One Plan Cannot Fit All Ministers

Ministers come in all shapes and sizes. Some are young; some are middle-aged. Some are nearing retirement; some are retired. Some are bivocational (many more than most people realize). Needs change and interests vary. A minister in a large city church will have concerns that are quite different from a pastor in a small village church.

But the varying needs often are a matter of degree, not substance. Housing, food, college costs, insurance protection, savings, writing a will, retirement provisions, investments, making a workable budget, automobile options—all have a key place in a minister's financial plan.

That a single plan cannot fit all ministers mandates planning. It calls for "your plan," not someone else's! Planning is absolutely imperative. Queen Victoria is reported to have snapped at her prime minister, Gladstone, when he told her she must sign some papers. "Don't ever use the word *must* to me. I despise it," she snarled. You may feel the same way without her imperiousness, but the truth remains that you *must* plan! You must develop *your* plan.

That plan must include short-range goals, medium-range goals, and long-range goals. Add to this the budget framework to move toward those goals. Then experience the early satisfaction of realized financial goals, and you will make basic financial planning a lifelong discipline.

Plan as a Family

Almost more important than the priority of planning is the necessity of involving the family in financial management. One obvious reason for this practice is that familial involvement allows children to develop management skills in handling their own money.

Most ministers have had to learn money management in spite of family noninvolvement or extremely poor examples from parents. More family fights center on money than on any other subject. The Christian family, and certainly a minister's family, should be exemplary in this area.

I am not advocating pure democracy in family financial planning. Giving children an equal vote with a parent is usually very unwise, but children need to understand the principles of income and expenses. They need to learn by handling allowances, keeping savings accounts, discussing the actual cost of operating a car or of going to college. Give each member of the family a voice in your decision-making process.

Family planning is multifaceted in the husband/wife balance. More ministers' wives are working because two incomes are often needed in a minister's family to make ends meet. How do families handle two incomes? Each family plans according to its individual needs and tastes. But please plan as a family. It can be one of the most rewarding aspects of family life.

Work Toward Owning Your Own Home

Ministers usually are quartered at sometime in their careers in church-owned housing. Occasionally, this is advantageous; more times than not, it is disadvantageous. Building an equity in a home, using the minister's tax-excluded housing allowance, enjoying the freedom of owning one's own home, and preparing a home for retirement years are some of the main reasons for this major goal of financial planning.

Often there are circumstances over which the minister has no control. Some churches simply will not get out of the housing business. Some lay leaders do not understand housing issues. Some ministers have abused the issue by demanding assistance with down payments.

Despite all of these factors, the goal is still eminently worthwhile. Housing is essential. Sooner or later, you and your wife will need your own home. Work toward it.

Keep a Cautious Eye on Your Credit and Debt

Dr. Samuel Johnson had a good point when he said, "Whatever you have, spend less!" That is good advice, but it is far easier to repeat these words than to put them into practice.

One of the best steps in successful money management is to drive some rules down deep. Get out of debt, and stay out of debt. Get to a cash basis as soon as possible. Some go so far as to make "cash only" the rule for every purchase. If you can operate this way, fine! I personally think there can be a few exceptions, such as a home, a car, or major appliances. The fewer the exceptions to cash only, the better manager you will be. The main rule is to avoid excessive credit charges, the trap of impulse buying because of the convenience of a credit card.

Interest charges in today's world are phenomenally high. They often are higher than the cost of the product. Train a cautious eye constantly on your debt ratio to cash income. Keep those monthly payments to a minimum. No more vicious idea ever was born than "the easy monthly payment." It has led untold numbers of families over the precipice of financial irresponsibility. "Buy now—pay later" is horrible advice.

The truth-in-lending laws passed in recent years make credit card issuers tell you what your balance costs. Charges of 20 percent interest are not uncommon. No wonder the stores want you to charge. Read the fine print. Move to a cash basis on food, clothing, recreation, and as many other areas of buying as quickly as possible.

Forget the Get-Rich-Quick Schemes in Investment

Why is it the preacher is susceptible to get-rich-quick schemes in investments? Can it be because of persuasive laypersons? Is it an ego trip? Or is it due to hidden desires for sudden wealth? Whatever the reason, some ministers have been mesmerized by stock offers, real estate speculations, and participation in franchise offers. A few have won the game, but many more are poorer and wiser.

If you have money to invest, remember that a good interest-bearing certificate of deposit, a savings account, or real estate which can appreciate are good vehicles. Stocks and bonds have good potential, but remember that most stock brokers live on their sales commissions. If the stock market appeals to your sense of investment challenge, go into this area with your parameters set for gain or loss if you can afford to lose.

Once more, let me say, forget the get-rich-quick schemes. Stick to basics!

Trust Your Denominational Plans and Products

You would expect me, as one who works for a denominational pension agency, to trumpet our products. Rather than that, let me emphasize our motivation, our concern, our experience in the insurance area, as well as in retirement annuities. The Annuity Board's motto is: "Serving those who serve the Lord." If we live up to that, our only reason for existing is to help you. My experience for years with most of America's major denominational pension boards confirms this conclusion.

I recall an association of churches which set up an organization to sell medical insurance to its pastors and families because of frustration with annual cost increases. A fine layman put the group together because he felt he could offer coverage through his firm at a lower cost. Thirty churches enrolled in the program.

Two years and two rounds of cost increases later, the Annuity Board received a plea for help from investors in the plan. Their coverage had been canceled. Just before cancellation, claims had been submitted for two heart bypass surgeries and also for a difficult, expensive premature birth. The company squeeze was complicated by eight pastoral changes and only three of the replacements wanting participation. None of the eight who moved could take their group insurance with them. Most of the group reenrolled in the denomination's plan after proving eligibility through the underwriting process.

To be sure, medical insurance is expensive, the cost increases constantly, and there are no bargains. Ministers must have this protection, even if it gravitates only to catastrophic coverage. You can trust your denomination not only to seek the best product at the best cost but also to be in business year after year.

I have often said facetiously that surely one of the by-products of heaven is to be in a place where medical insurance is not needed. It is a difficult part of the Annuity Board's work, and it is even more difficult to communicate our motives in trying to "Serve those who serve the Lord." I honestly believe you can trust your denomination.

Draw Up Your Own Blueprint for Retirement

Retirement for the minister can represent an unprecedented period of freedom and fulfillment. Beforehand, a minister's life is seldom his own. Often pressured by relentless meetings, funeral demands, insensitive congregations, and the stress of endless sermonic preparations, the minister and his family know little unscheduled time for planned personal activities.

Retirement is an unusual opportunity for the minister if the blueprint for financial planning is in place. There will be time for travel, family fellowships, development of hobbies, reading, and volunteer ministries. Retirement may mean a move to a cherished new home in a new location near children, a term of overseas mission service, or an interim pastoral ministry.

The keys to freedom in retirement are simple, necessitating a personal blueprint with (1) money enough to live on comfortably; (2) reasonably good health; and (3) the old adage of retirement *from* something *to* something. In other words, have a specific purpose in retirement. Put the three keys together, and you have an open door to freedom and fulfillment.

Keep Informed About Financial Issues

I hope these pages have stressed the conclusion that you do not have to be an expert to manage your financial affairs wisely. It takes care, common sense, and an understanding of your limitations. You can organize your financial affairs in an efficient, rewarding way to avoid costly, embarrassing, unnecessary blunders. You can know enough about the things you buy to get your money's worth. You can know enough to make sensible decisions about how you use your money, making certain that your income and expenses meet your budget plans.

Maintaining this balance demands that you stay informed about financial issues, such as inflation, timely investments, shopping values, trends in the market place, sources of loans, and college scholarships. The list is endless, but like it or not, you must handle money wisely. You will find an enhanced reputation at home and in your churches if you do it well.

Part of your Christian commitment requires you to be a good steward, which is just another way of saying you must be a good manager of your personal finances. You can do it!

Suggested Resources

Reasons abound for making financial planning in the minister's family an ongoing project. Endless resources are available for continued study. Listed below are some of them. Make your own list, but make this study a priority. It can be fascinating and interesting. Above all, it can be very helpful.

Books

Consumer Guide. *Your Retirement—A Complete Planning Guide.* New York: A. and W. Publishers, 1981. I referred to this paperback book in chapter 8. It is readable, practical, and brimming with additional resource material. I commend this to those concerned with retirement questions.

Davis, Lee E. *In Charge: Managing Money for Christian Living.* Nashville: Broadman Press, 1984. This book is an excellent resource to help families with money management process.

MacGregor, Malcolm. *Your Money Matters.* Minneapolis: Bethany House Publishers, 1980. This is an interesting volume with many anecdotes written from a Christian perspective. You may not agree with some of the philosophical opinions, but the practical advice is worth considering.

Pearce, J. Winston. *Ten Good Things I Know About Retirement.* Nashville: Broadman Press, 1982. Every preacher, regardless of age, should read this well-written, refreshing volume. It will whet the appetite for retirement. Even more, it will help you understand every retired person to whom you minister.

Porter, Sylvia. *New Money for the 80's*. Garden City, N. Y.: Doubleday and Co., 1979. Check this one out from your public library. It is big and expensive, but it is a good basic volume loaded with helpful suggestions about all subjects related to money and money management.

Stillman, Richard J. *Guide to Personal Finance: A Lifetime Program of Money Management*. Church Town, N. J.: Prentice Hall, 1980.

Governmental Publications

Superintendent of Documents
U. S. Printing Office
Washington, D. C. 20402

This government office issues all kinds of publications at low cost. It is one of the best sources in the country. Write for a listing, specifying your particular interest. The Agriculture Department also has good publications about food, nutrition, and so forth. Write:

> Publication Division
> Office of Communication
> U. S. Department of Agriculture
> Washington, D. C. 20250

Consumer Information Center
Pueblo, Colorado 81009

This is a good source of government publications. Write the department for a free catalog.

Nationwide Organization

All of these organizations will send you publications on request. Some are free; most are reasonably priced.

Bureau of Consumer Protection
Federal Trade Commission
6 Pennsylvania Avenue, N. W.
Washington, DC 20580

Consumers Union
256 Washington Street
Mount Vernon, NY 10553

Council of Better Business Bureaus
1515 Wilson Boulevard, Suite 300
Arlington, VA 22209

Office of Consumer Affairs
Premier Building, Room 1003
1725 Eye Street, N.W.
Washington, DC 20201

Associated Credit Bureaus, Inc.
P.O. Box 218300
Houston, TX 77218

Social Security

Social Security Administration
6401 Security Boulevard
Baltimore, MD 21235

Veterans Benefits

Veterans Administration
941 North Capitol Street, N.E.
Washington, DC 20421

Agencies for the Needs of Aging Citizens

United States Administration of Aging
330 Independence, S.W.
Washington, DC 20202

Social and Rehabilitation Service
330 C Street, S. W. — Room 3090
Washington, DC 20202

Health and Human Services Department
200 Independence, S. W.
Washington, DC 20201

National Council on the Aging, Inc.
600 Maryland Avenue, S. W.
West Wing 100
Washington, DC 20024

National Council of Senior Citizens
925 15th Street, N. W.
Washington, DC 20005

Senate Special Committee on Aging
Dirksen Building—Room G33
Washington, DC 20510

American Association of Retired Persons
1909 K Street, N. W.
Washington, DC 20049

National Health Care Organizations

American Medical Association
535 North Dearborn Street
Chicago, IL 60610

American Dental Association
211 East Chicago Avenue
Chicago, IL 60611

American Public Health Association
1015 — 15th Street
Washington, DC 20005

National Medical Association
1012 — 10th Street, N. W.
Washington, DC 20001

United States Public Health Service
5600 Fishers Lane
Rockville, MD 20852

American Hospital Association
840 North Lake Shore Drive
Chicago, IL 60611

Health Research Group
2000 P Street, N. W., Suite 700
Washington, DC 20036

Life Insurance

American Council of Life Insurance
1850 K Street, N. W. — Suite 600
Washington, DC 20006

Financial Publications

Barron's
22 Cortland Street
New York, NY 10007

Better Investing
Box 220
Royal Oak, MI 48068

Financial Weekly
Media General
P.O. Box C-32333
Richmond, VA 23293

Financial World
1450 Broadway
New York, NY 10018

Forbes
60 Fifth Avenue
New York, NY 10011

Money
c/o Time Life Building
Rockefeller Center
New York, NY 10020

The Wall Street Journal
22 Cortland Street
New York, NY 100007

If you do not want to subscribe to these publications, get them from your public library.

APPENDIX
Minister's Data Checklist

This Check List was compiled or updated in _____.

(Mo. Yr.)

All important documents are kept in _____.

We have a safe deposit box in _____.

Box No. _____. Key No. _____. The key is kept in _____.

Persons authorized to open safe deposit box: _____.

Personal Information

MYSELF
Full Name _____ Birthdate _____
Place of Birth _____ Social Security No. _____
Ordination Date and Place _____

Date   Place

Present Address _____ City _____
Residence State _____ Zip _____ Date of Res. in This State _____

MY SPOUSE
Maiden Name _____ Date of Marriage _____
Previous Marriage, if any _____ Maiden Name _____
Date of Marriage _____ Date Terminated _____
Reason: Death _____ Divorce _____

CHILDREN
Name and Birthdate of Each Child:

_____ _____
_____ _____
_____ _____
_____ _____
_____ _____

OTHER IMMEDIATE RELATIVES

_____
_____
_____

WILLS AND PERSONS TO CONTACT
My Will is Dated as of _____ 19____
My Will is Located in _____
My Spouse's Will is Dated as of _____ 19____
My Spouse's Will is Located in _____

Executor(s) of My Estate Are:

_____
_____
_____

Persons to Notify at My Death:

_____
_____
_____

Key Advisors to Me and My Family to Be Notified:

Accountant _____ Telephone _____
Address _____

Attorney _____ Telephone _____
Address _____

Banker _____ Telephone _____
Address _____

Broker _____ Telephone _____
Address _____

Denominational Office _____ Telephone _____
Address _____

Church Leader _____ Telephone _____
Address _____

Insurance Agent(s) _____ Telephone _____
Address _____

Minister _____ Telephone _____
Church _____
Address _____

Physician(s) _____ Telephone _____
Address _____

Trust Officer _____ Telephone _____
Address _____

Other _____ Telephone _____
Address _____

IMPORTANT DOCUMENTS AND PERSONAL PAPERS

	What They Are	*Where They Are Kept*

CERTIFICATES AND PAPERS
Marriage _____
Birth _____
Citizenship _____
Adoption of Children _____
Divorce or Separation _____
Other _____

MILITARY SERVICE
Branch _____ Rank _____
Discharge _____ Date _____
Honors and Commendations _____

SOCIAL SECURITY CARDS
My Number _____
My Spouse's Number _____

EMPLOYMENT RECORDS
Church and Denominational
For Me _____
For Spouse _____

Secular
For Me _____
For Spouse _____

ORGANIZATIONS, OFFICES AND DATES
Denominational _____
_____
_____
Fraternal _____
Union _____
Other _____

AUTOMOBILE(S) REGISTRATION

_____

_____

EDUCATION RECORDS
Diploma(s) _____
Dissertation(s) _____
Other _____

                    What They Are   *Where They Are Kept*

MEDICAL RECORDS
Allergies _____
Special Medication(s) _____
Vaccinations _____
Other _____

FUNERAL AND BURIAL
Burial Lot(s) Location _____
Burial Lot(s) Deed of Sale _____
Donation of Body, Organs _____
Funeral Instruction _____

_____

BUSINESS AND PROPERTY
Tax Returns
Income Tax _____
State and Local _____
Real Estate _____
Other _____

Property
Deeds and Abstracts of Titles _____

_____

Retirement
Plan Contracts _____
Agency to Contact _____
Other _____

Household Inventory
(List of all items, dates purchased, prices for major items)

_____

Special Possessions
Furs _____
Jewelry _____
Electronic and Photographic _____

Collections (Stamps, Money, etc.) _____

Credit Cards and Charge Accounts (List by name and number)
_____
_____
_____

Warranties and Guarantees
_____

	What They Are	*Where They Are Kept*

Home Accounting
Receipts _____
Records _____
Keys _____
Instructions _____
Other _____

FINANCIAL ACCOUNTS

Firm	*Address* *Banks*	*Account Number*	*Location of Papers*

Savings and Loan

U.S. SAVINGS BONDS OWNED
Location _____

Serial Number	*Name and Beneficiary*	*Date Bought*	*Amount Paid*	*Maturity Date and Value*

BONDS, STOCKS, OTHERS
Location _____

Company	Serial No.	No. Shares	Date Bought	Cost of Shares

MOTOR VEHICLES
Type _____
Location of Papers _____
Loans Against _____

REAL ESTATE
Property Location _____
_____

Deed Location _____
Miscellaneous _____

CHURCH AND DENOMINATIONAL
Name of Church Pension Board _____
Address _____ Telephone _____
City _____ State _____ Zip Code _____
My Personal Member Number _____

Type of Protection	Member Number	Premium	Total Value
Retirement Plan(s)			
Insurance			
Disability			
Hospital			
Major Medical			
Life			

NONDENOMINATIONAL INSURANCE

Type	Agent and Co.	Policy No.	Benefits	Premium Cost	Due Date
Life					
Medical					
Accident					
Auto					
Home					
Liability					

Other   _____   _____   _____   _____   _____

DEBTS WE OWE
Amount   Type   Payment Amount and Date   To Whom Owed   Maturity Date

_____

_____

DEBTS OWED US
Amount   Type   Payment Amount and Date   To Whom Owed   Maturity Date

_____

_____

OTHER BUSINESS OR PERSONAL
Amount   Type   Payment Amount and Date   To Whom Owed   Maturity Date

_____

_____

Data Updated as of _____
                         Month   Day   Year

_____

My Signature